SOUTH AFRICA AND THE EUROPEAN UNION

About the author

Professor Gerrit Olivier holds a PhD-degree in International Politics from the University of Pretoria, South Africa. He was a senior lecturer in Politics at the University of Zululand and professor of International Relations at the Rand Afrikaans University (now University of Johannesburg), as well as the University of Pretoria. He joined the South African diplomatic service in 1983 and served as head of the first South African diplomatic mission to the Soviet Union (1991). Olivier was appointed as South Africa's first ambassador to the Russian Federation and the Republic of Kazakhstan (1992–1996). He is presently Director of the Centre for European Studies at the University of Johannesburg and professor (extraordinary) at the Department of Political Sciences, University of Pretoria.

SOUTH AFRICA AND THE
EUROPEAN UNION
SELF-INTEREST, IDEOLOGY AND ALTRUISM

GERRIT OLIVIER

Protea Book House
Pretoria
2006

TO EMILY, MICHÈLE, TANYA AND ANTON-LOUIS

South Africa and the European Union:
Self-interest, Ideology and Altruism

First edition, first impression 2006

Protea Book House
PO Box 35110, Menlo Park, 0102
1067 Burnett Street, Hatfield, 0083
protea@intekom.co.za

Typography and design by Ada Radford
Cover design by Hond CC
Printed and bound by Paarl Print

ISBN 10: 1-86919-139-0
ISBN 13: 978-1-86919-139-9

© 2006 Gerrit Olivier
© All rights reserved.
No part of this book may be reproduced without the permission of the publisher.

Contents

List of abbreviations	6
Preface	9
1. Europe's role in the shaping of South Africa: An overview	13
2. Europe and apartheid South Africa: The parting of ways	24
3. South Africa's foreign policy and national interests in the context of the European Union's international role	35
4. The evolution of the European Union's development policy	45
5. The European Union's policy towards democratic South Africa	57
6. Benevolence and self-interest in the European Union's policy towards South Africa	84
7. The regional context of South African/European Union/African relations	93
8. The European Union and NEPAD: From failed promises to partnership	141
9. An assessment of European Union policy towards South Africa	154
Postscript	170
Selected Bibliography	175
Index	181

For easy reference, this text will use the term "European Union" (EU) throughout unless it is contextually necessary to refer to its earlier titles, namely the European Economic Community (EEC) and the European Community (EC).

List of abbreviations

ACP	African, Caribbean and Pacific countries
ANC	African National Congress
APRM	African Peer Review Mechanism
AU	African Union
BLNS	Botswana, Lesotho, Namibia and Swaziland
CADSP	Common African Defence and Security Policy
CAP	Common Agricultural Policy
CBI	Cross-Border Initiative
CE	Council of Europe
CEAO	Communité Economique de l'Afrique de l'Ouest
CFSP	Common Foreign and Security Policy
CMA	Common Monetary Area
COMESA	Common Market of Eastern and Southern Africa
Coreper	Committee of Permanent Representatives
Cosatu	Congress of South African Trade Unions
CWCI	Conference, Workshop and Cultural Initiative Fund
DMS	Development Merchant System
EAPC	Euro-Atlantic Partnership Council
EBRD	European Bank for Reconstruction and Development
EC	European Community
ECA	Economic Commission for Africa
ECOWAS	Economic Community of West African States
ECSC	European Coal and Steel Community
ECU	European Currency Unit
EDF	European Development Fund
EEC	European Economic Community
EESC	European Economic and Social Committee
EIB	European Investment Bank
EMS	European Monetary System
EMU	European Economic and Monetary Union
EPA	Economic Partnership Agreement
EPRD	European Programme for Reconstruction and Development
ERM	Exchange Rate Mechanism
ESDP	European Security and Defence Policy
ESS	European Security Strategy
EU	European Union
Euratom	European Atomic Energy Community
FDI	Foreign Direct Investment
FTA	Free Trade Agreement
GNP	Gross National Product

GNU	Government of National Unity
G7	Group of Seven Industrialised Nations
G8	Group of Seven Industrialised Nations plus Russia
IMF	International Monetary Fund
JSTCC	Joint Science and Technology Cooperation Committee
MDG	Millennium Development Goal
MIP	Multi-annual Indicative Programme
NAFTA	North American Free Trade Agreement
NAM	Non-Aligned Movement
NATO	North Atlantic Treaty Organisation
NEPAD	New Partnership for Africa's Development
OAU	Organisation for African Unity
ODA	Official Development Assistance
OSCE	Organisation for Security and Cooperation in Europe
PAP	Pan-African Parliament
QMV	Qualified Majority Voting
RDP	Reconstruction and Development Programme
RRF	Rapid Reaction Force
SA	South Africa
SACP	South African Communist Party
SACU	Southern African Customs Union
SADCC	Southern African Development Coordination Conference
SADC	Southern African Development Community
SAP	Structural Adjustment Programme
SEA	Single European Act
SEM	Single European Market
SME	Small and Medium-sized Enterprises
STABEX	System of Stabilisation of Export Earnings
SYSMIN	System to Stabilize ACP Countries' Earnings from Mining
TABEISA	Technical and Business Education Initiative of South Africa
TB	Tuberculosis
TDCA	Trade, Development and Cooperation Agreement
TEC	Treaty of the European Community
TEU	Treaty of the European Union
UDEAC	Union Douanière et Economique de l'Afrique Centrale
UDF	United Democratic Front
UK	United Kingdom
UN	United Nations
US	United States
VAT	Value-Added Tax
WEU	Western European Union
WTO	World Trade Organisation

Preface

In 1994, South Africa's 342 year old epoch of Eurocentric values made way for a new era of Afrocentrism. The impact of this transformation on the South African political culture and the perceptions of decision makers was obviously profound. This was especially true with regards to the country's foreign policy, which began to concentrate more specifically on Africa, the Southern hemisphere and the developing world in general. Europe was no longer at the apex of South Africa's foreign policy hierarchy. Though the European influence was not totally disregarded, it was superseded by new interests, objectives and ideological predilections that moved from the previous close cultural and political ties to an economic basis. This new economic relationship was epitomised by the conclusion of a Trade, Development and Cooperation Agreement in 1999. Today, the EU is South Africa's biggest trading partner as well as the biggest donor of development aid to the country. Even so, these amicable relations have never developed into what may be called a "special relationship". But with the ever increasing importance of economic diplomacy as part of countries' foreign policy, this might change soon.

Europe, and the EU in particular, is of primary importance to South Africa, from both a political and economic perspective. Because the EU is not a state or nation but a complex, multilateral organisation with many dimensions, it is often not understood in South Africa. This book has been written in an attempt to cast more light on the EU and its importance in South Africa. Hopefully, it will also encourage South Africans to take more interest in the relationship between these two parties and to become involved in the intellectual and policy-related debate surrounding it.

I wish to thank the University of Johannesburg, particularly the dean of the Faculty of Arts, Professor Rory Ryan, and the chairperson of the Department of Politics and Government, Professor Yolanda Sadie, for allowing me the time and resources to complete this book. I am grateful to Maureen Dry, who did such a splendid job in helping me to get the manuscript ready for print, and also the publishers, Protea Book House, for their unfailingly professional and patient support. Finally, thank you to Emily for the encouragement and for waiting so patiently for the completion of the book.

Gerrit Olivier

The empires of the future are the empires of the mind.
　　　　　　　　– *Winston Churchill* –

Chapter 1
Europe's role in the shaping of South Africa: An overview

Introduction

South Africa's connection with Europe dates back to the discovery of the sea route around the Cape by the Portuguese navigator Bartholomeu Dias in 1487 and, more particularly, the establishment of a Dutch settlement at the Cape of Good Hope in 1652. Since then, European involvement has shaped the modern future of South Africa like no other single outside force. For a considerable period of its existence, South Africa was, culturally speaking, "part of Europe in Africa", with European norms and values playing a dominant role in the development and modernization processes of the country's political, economic, administrative and social systems.

With the introduction of majority rule in South Africa in 1994, the Eurocentric epoch finally came to an end and South African policies and political affinities became predominantly Afrocentric.[1] As a result, in the political lexicon of South Africa's new rulers, Eurocentric values were deemed as being alien and intrusive to Africa and the African value system.[2] However, the ruling

---
1 See particularly in this regard Thabo Mbeki's "I am an African" speech before the South African Parliament on 8 May 1996, (published as occasional paper, Konrad Adenauer Stiftung, Johannesburg, May 1998, pp. 5–7), and his address "Africa's time has come", (The Corporate Council Summit at Chantilly, Virginia, US, April 1997).
2 Even so, the trend in Africa seems to be shifting. Zimbabwe's President Robert Mugabe slammed "the majority" of his counterparts in Africa, saying that they had succumbed to Western influence and turned against African issues. "They are oriented towards the West, not oriented towards Africa, towards their own people, not nationalistic in the true sense of the word." Quoted in *Pretoria News*, 25 February 2004, p. 5.

African National Congress (ANC) admitted in its 2005 discussion paper that "in a country with many languages, religions and ethnic groups, the national question will always be with us".[3] Even so, "Africanisation" remains an important ideological objective of the government that took over from a previously white, Eurocentric and predominantly Afrikaner ruling class. In the discussion paper it was clearly suggested that whites should transform their European or Western identity in favour of an African identity in order to become more acceptable in the new South Africa. Using the Afrikaners as an example, the document stated: "Do [the Afrikaners] have to be in Africa for another hundred years before they are considered African?" and "it is becoming clearer and clearer that white Afrikaners have a different emotional, psychological and material relationship to Africa and SA compared with other whites".

Africanisation, as applied to South Africans from European origin, therefore seems to be used in the context of the transformation from a European identity to an African identity and a switch from emotional/cultural identification with Europe to identification with Africa. Bearing in mind, however, the omnipresence and dominant functional role of Western values and typically Western manifestations of modernization and modernity in virtually all walks of public life among South Africa's entire population, both black and white, this transformation, while ideologically salient in the current political climate, seems incongruent with prevailing reality. Actually, while the South African society is multifragmented and multicultural, it is dominated by an overarching syncretic Afro-European value system, culture and economic and behavioural practices. Moreover, these orientations coincide or blend with what could be called a "universal culture", defined as "the increasing acceptance of common values, beliefs, orientations, practices and institutions by peoples throughout the world".[4] Although the South African *political culture and style* have become predominantly Afrocentric since 1994, the *operative* or *functional* culture, i.e. legal, administrative, economic, technological and recreational, remains broadly European or Westernized. At the same time, English has become the *lingua franca* of the South African nation as well as of the black dominated government and the new black elite. There is no doubt, however, that with the passage of time the national

---

3   J. Burtenshaw, "Afrikaners are embracing the new South Africa", *Beeld*, 25 May 2005, p. 14.
4   S. P. Huntington, *The clash of civilizations and the remaking of world order* (New York, Simon & Shuster, 1996), p. 56.

value system and ethos of South Africans will increasingly shift to become more typically and essentially African.

In spite of these blurred, overlapping aspects of South Africa's cultural identity, an important shift from one epoch to another has taken place since 1994 in terms of the national power configuration, the dominant value system, the mode of governance, cultural identification and political/ideological preferences. All these followed on South Africa's finally becoming "part of Africa" after 342 years. The apartheid curtain that previously divided South Africa from the rest of the continent made way for a new spirit of *ubuntu*: African fraternity, African unity, and intra-African cooperation in the policy making of the new government. At the same time, Afrocentrism replaced Eurocentrism as the central ideology shaping South Africa's foreign policy. The emotional, ideological and political texture of the relationship with Europe therefore changed and the special relationship that existed for most of the 20th century came to an end. Although the West, Europe, and the European Union in particular, remained an important focus of South Africa's foreign policy, its main trading partner and source of wealth creation, investment, tourism and development aid, these relations have become more distant, more businesslike and more competitive, guided by necessity and self-interest rather than emotional affinity. This new relationship is, of course, not exactly the preferred situation from the European Union's (EU) point of view. It has consistently attempted to draw South Africa closer into a new special relationship or partnership by way of lucrative development assistance programmes, a Free Trade Agreement (FTA), and sustained diplomatic efforts over a broad spectrum. Although such a relationship would certainly be in South Africa's own long-term interest, historical and cultural fault lines between Europe and Africa seem to stand in the way.

The good and the bad of early European involvement in South Africa

European involvement in South Africa went through various phases over a period of 350 years, each of these leaving an indelible imprint in the development and future of the country and its peoples (see box 1).

The beginning of European involvement in South Africa was small, inconspicuous and even insignificant, but it was a beginning that set off powerful historical forces that have to this day not settled into a permanent equilibrium. Despite the relatively

BOX 1   IMPORTANT EPOCHS AND EVENTS IN SOUTH AFRICAN HISTORY SINCE ITS EUROPEAN DISCOVERY

- Discovery by Portuguese navigator Bartholomeu Dias (1487)
- Occupation of the Cape of Good Hope by the Dutch East Indian Company (1652)
- Settlement of European immigrant farmers in the Cape (1652)
- The Cape administered by the Dutch East Indian Company as an agricultural settlement (1652–1795)
- British temporary rule of the Cape (1795–1803)
- The Cape under the rule of the Batavian Republic (Dutch) (1803–1806)
- Colonial status under Britain (1806–1910)
- The discovery of diamonds (1867) and gold (1886) in South Africa and the influx of European entrepreneurs and fortune seekers
- Manifestations of British imperialism and colonial greed after the discovery of gold and diamonds culminating in the three year Anglo-Boer War and the British colonisation of the northern Boer republics (1899–1902)
- Unification of South Africa and dominion status under British colonial rule (1910)
- Self-governing status under the British Crown and member of the British Commonwealth (1926)
- Sovereign independence from Britain (1934)
- Military cooperation between South Africa and the Allied powers during World Wars 1 and 2
- The apartheid era under National Party rule and the beginning of South Africa's international isolation (1948–1994)
- The formation of the Republic of South Africa (1961)
- South Africa's withdrawal from the Commonwealth (1961)
- Majority rule in South Africa, the normalization of relations with European countries and the start of a relationship with the European Union (1994–)
- Entering into a Trade, Development and Cooperation Agreement (TDCA) with the EU and qualified membership of the Cotonou Partnership Agreement (2000)

small influx of European settlers, mainly from the Netherlands, France and Britain, their influence, both good and bad, was lasting, profound and complex. On the one hand, they were the early modernisers and pioneers; on the other hand, they were also exploiters and the harbingers of a perennial racial problem and a political division between black and white that has stayed with South Africa until today. From the very beginning after the establishment of the Dutch East Indian Company's halfway station at the Cape of Good Hope in 1652, the relationship between European settlers and the native inhabitants of the country was generally adversarial. Hostility and clashes between the settlers and the native inhabitants in the Cape followed very much the same pattern as that of European settlement in North America, Australia and New Zealand: conflict over *Lebensraum*, land, livestock and other earthly possessions. At the same time, the relationship between the settlers and their colonial overlords was also tense and uneasy and periodically even hostile, to such an extent that a sizable portion of the Dutch speaking population joined the Great Trek to the North in the 1830s to escape the repressive colonial regime of the British.

South African history turned out very different to most of the other former European colonies' because in South Africa, native inhabitants were not massively and systematically exterminated and enslaved, as was the case, for instance, with the North and South American Indians, the Congolese under Belgian rule, and the Australian Aborigines. As a permanent and inescapable part of the South African reality, they had to be accommodated politically in one way or another, although discrimination, racist cruelty, cultural and economic disownment and exploitation did play a major role in the accommodation process. In early South Africa, as in the abovementioned colonies, it was an unequal struggle, mainly because of the wide discrepancy between a more modern, military superior European settler society and the military weak, technologically backward and divided and dispersed local tribes. This was a situation in which colonialism could flourish, as it indeed did in South Africa until the beginning of the 20th century. However, change was inevitable. Although repression and discrimination continued for more than three centuries, the struggle between black and white about political power, majority rule, political rights, democracy and equal constitutional and civil rights finally ended in a victory for the predominantly black ANC majority in 1994.

The European influence and role affected the indigenous population in multiple ways. The instruments of this influence were the policies and practices of successive colonial administrations, Christian schools, churches and missionaries, and modern agricultural, economic, administrative, commercial, legal and other professional procedures. The South African indigenous population adapted to alternative modern European cultural behavioural patterns, some of their own choice, but the majority because of existential economic necessity. In most cases, the new Western culture did not replace the traditional African culture in a zero-sum fashion, but existed as a parallel culture, particularly for those who participated in the new emerging market economy. In the case of the modernising upwardly mobile urbanised Africans, the acculturation process was more profound, leading to the formation of a unique cultural mix among them and the emergence of a putative Euro-African civilization. The transference of European values and European technological skills and innovations to the indigenous South African population over a period of almost four centuries resulted in the profound cultural and economic transformation towards modernity of the African proletariat. It affected the permanent acceptance of the Western forms, style and practices of national politics and statecraft, bureaucracy, economic models, administration of justice, and sport. Because of these developments, the country, although seriously blighted by the policy of apartheid, emerged in the 20th century as the strongest in Africa and a competitive role player in global politics and economics. It is not the intention and place to here argue the merits and demerits of colonialism, which is a vast subject on its own and a very complicated, multidimensional, emotional and unfinished debate.[5] For the purpose of this analysis, the point could be made, however, that much of the clamour about the discrepancy between rich and poor, developed and underdeveloped, modernization and the lack thereof, has to do with the inadequate transfer of development assistance, technology and direct investment from the rich industrialised nations of the Northern hemisphere to the poor developing nations of the Southern hemisphere. The current political catchphrase used to legitimise this type of assistance is "partnership". In terms of contents, philosophy and morality alone there are, of course, a vast difference between colonialism, neo-colonialism and partnership. Broadly speaking, however, from a developmental and modernization point of view, they address the same subject in their own particular way.

The Portuguese did not colonise the Cape after Dias's discovery of the sea route. In 1652 the Dutch East Indian Company occupied it as a halfway station to supply victuals to their trade ships on the Far East route. Formal colonisation under the Netherlands government (Batavian Republic) only took place for

---

5   See, for instance, D. D'Souza, "Two cheers for colonialism", *Mail and Guardian*, 10–16 May 2002, pp. 30–31; J. Matshikiza, "A colonised intellect", *Mail and Guardian*, 17–22 May 2002, pp. 28–29.

a brief period at the turn of the 18th century (1803–1806, following temporary British rule from 1795–1803); thereafter the British occupied and colonised the Cape in 1806. After the Anglo-Boer War (1899–1902), Britain also annexed the Boer republics of the Orange Free State and Transvaal, converting the entire present-day South Africa into a British colony. When Britain agreed to the formation of the new Union of South Africa in 1910 as a dominion within the Commonwealth, it also agreed with the South African National Convention's compromise on voting rights, which meant that the *status quo* pertaining to the previous separate colonies could be maintained and that a "Union of Whites" could effectively be established. In doing so, Britain wittingly participated in setting the scene for white exclusivism and white domination in South Africa for years to come.[6] However, the European settlers and their colonial masters gained the political upper hand over the indigenous population only temporarily, and at the turn of the 20th century, the actual political power finally shifted from the white to the black population.

The collapse of British colonialist and white hegemony in South Africa was inevitable. Of course, it took a long time – more than a hundred years – for British colonialism in South Africa to move from apex to zenith. Although British imperialism prevailed in the Anglo-Boer War, the victory was in many respects a pyrrhic one, as the writing was already on the wall: colonialism would become an unsustainable anachronism. Moreover, in the wake of their victory in 1902, the colonial overlords also failed to correctly read the directions of change in South Africa. Instead of preparing the way for the inevitable, i.e. majority rule, they chose to hand over power in 1910 to a white ruling class, hoping that this arrangement would serve their own interests better. Britain, therefore, probably deserves more blame than praise for the way it shaped the future of South Africa, particularly for its policy of imperialist greed and exploitation and its being instrumental in the denial of equal political rights to all South Africans in colonial times. This policy largely set the scene for the rise of Afrikaner nationalism, racist hegemony, and the apartheid policy of the National Party after 1948.

The post-independent white regime succeeded admirably in maintaining amicable relations with Britain and safeguarding

---

6 South Africa was not an exceptional manifestation of discrimination under British colonial rule. For instance, discrimination of a similar kind was applicable to "untouchables" in India where a British policy of separate electoral privileges applied. See in this regard, S. Wolpert, *Gandhi's passion: The life and legacy of Mahatma Gandhi* (Oxford, Oxford University Press, 2001), Chapter 16.

and reinforcing cultural ties with Europe. However, after the victory of Afrikaner nationalism under the banner of the National Party in 1948, these ties were progressively contaminated by apartheid and South Africa's consequent international pariahdom. Eventually Britain had no choice but to turn its back on what was partly its own creation. This was also the beginning of the end for any sort of special relationship between Europe and the most westernized country in Africa south of the Sahara. Although the National Party government tried to maintain a special relationship with European nations, using arguments like kith and kin connections, the strategic importance for the West of the Cape sea route, the country's mineral wealth, and South Africa's being a bastion against Communist expansion, it was all in vain.

The release of Nelson Mandela from prison in 1990 was a watershed event unequalled by any other in South African history. It finally signalled the end of an era for South African/ European relations. The ANC government that came into power in 1994 showed scant emotional and cultural affinity towards Europe, preferring to be guided by the doctrines of Afro-centrism, pan-Africanism and non-alignment.[7] Later, Eurocentric manifestations of special political and cultural bilateral relationships were replaced by a foreign policy reflecting a cordial but more distant association dominated by mundane economic interests. The caveat should be added, however, that the ANC's public disparagement of Eurocentrism was probably more a matter of ideological expediency than inner conviction, and that a difference should be drawn between its anti-Eurocentric rhetoric and its practical actions. In reality, the transaction flow between South Africa and Europe, including regular high profile official visits by leaders, has increased steeply since 1994. Indeed, European capitals have become a preferred destination of the new breed of South African politicians and bureaucrats. With the establishment of the new democratic South Africa, the EU (formerly the European Economic Community (EEC) and the European Community (EC)) emerged as a more important role player in the country's relations with Europe than was previously the case, placing these relations on a different footing and with more emphasis on the economic rather than the ideological-emotional dimensions.

Looking beyond the well-chronicled ill effects of colonialism, European involvement in the nascent South African state also

---

7   See G. Olivier, "Is Thabo Mbeki Africa's saviour?", *International Affairs*, 79:4 (July 2003), pp. 815–828.

had a positive dimension. Most significant in this respect were the profound and far-reaching processes of development, the modernization that took place under European influence, the laying of the foundations for an industrialized, free-market economic system in South Africa, as well as the development of a modern physical infrastructure and financial and legal networks in the country. From the anti-colonial perspective, it could be argued that the process of development and modernization came at too high a price when taking into account the exploitation of the country's abundant natural resources, the use of slave labour in the beginning and later of cheap local black labour, and the disruptive acculturation process among the indigenous population who had no choice but to conform to the European cultural model of civilization. Of course, this process was not unique to South Africa. With or without the aberrations of colonialism, the global impact of westernization has been ubiquitous and inevitable since the 17th century.[8] In fact, since ancient history the domination of and exploitation by the strong over the weak has been a regular feature of human existence. Very few societies escaped the bitter fate of foreign invasion and domination. It was only after World War 2 that this sort of political action, today called colonialism, became morally intolerable and was dispensed with as unacceptable political behaviour.

Although broadly similar consequences resulted from European involvement elsewhere in Africa, its impact on South Africa's future was unquestionably the most profound. Among the reasons for South Africa's prominence were the relative importance of South Africa to the trading nations and maritime powers in Europe because of the strategic value of the sea route around the Cape of Good Hope; the relatively large number of Europeans who over the years had settled permanently in South Africa; the abundance of mineral wealth in the South African soil, particularly that of strategic minerals like gold, platinum and diamonds, which attracted investors, entrepreneurs, developers, intellectuals, and fortune seekers of all kinds; and the substantial direct capital investment in the South African economy made by European countries, the United Kingdom in particular.

In summary, therefore, European involvement had two main overarching dimensions, namely an exploitative one and a developmental one. It was exploitative in the sense that a high price was exacted from successive generations of black South Africans because of both institutionalised and informal racial and political inequality and economic mistreatment. On the develop-

---

8 See Huntington, *The clash of civilizations*, chapter 8.

mental side, South Africa's development and modernization reached an unparalleled level of sophistication in the African context and today it is by a very wide margin the strongest military, industrial and economic power on the African continent. To an important extent, South Africa escaped the plight of other sub-Saharan African states that went through a painful process under colonialism of superficial westernization without technological modernization.

This strong impact of European influence on South Africa lasted until the end of World War 2, when it became more remote and indirect. The decline of the power status of the colonial powers, the emergence of Afrikaner nationalism, the international politics of the Cold War and East/West competition, as well as the proliferation of liberation movements in colonial territories precipitated the end of colonialism and the end of Europe's special relations with South Africa. At the same time, issues like national self-determination, racism and human rights acquired global saliency. In South Africa, this trend was opposed and contradicted by the National Party victory in the 1948 general elections, which set the scene for an inevitable process of alienation between Europe and South Africa.

Conclusion

For a major part of South African modern history – almost 300 years – European influence was predominantly represented and promoted by the Netherlands and Britain as occupiers and colonial rulers. The political relations between local settlers, native South Africans and the colonial regimes were generally adversarial and even confrontational and violent. On cultural, technological and economic levels, European presence and rule left a profound and lasting impact: South Africa developed and modernised according to European economic and technological standards, adopted European cultural and behavioural patterns, and the country evolved into the most modernised and powerful state in Africa. But all this came at a high price. The socio-political legacy left by the colonial powers in the nascent South Africa was that of a house divided under white minority rule. Racial and ethnic divisions were politicised and institutionalised and while a special privileged political and economic status accrued to the white population, their black compatriots were generally discriminated against and were excluded from the national political and economic reward system and equal citizenship. Predictably, this policy became a hotbed for growing black resentment, racial cleavages and political divisions and polarisation, a recipe for future conflict and disaster.

What the colonial regime did was to reap the benefits of their exploitation and to leave the responsibility to future generations of South Africans to deal with a potentially explosive situation. This situation could probably have been averted by more prescient and sensible policies while the colonial regime was still in power. After British rule, the white minority to whom the power was handed simply carried on according to past practices in order to secure its own survival and supremacy. To an important extent, therefore, the policy of apartheid was an ideological and intellectual derivative of early European influences that manifested not only in South Africa, but also elsewhere in Africa where European colonies existed. South Africa became the slave of its history. For a considerable period after British colonialism had ended in South Africa, the former rulers went on to maintain special friendly and cosy relations with the local white minority government. It was only after the devastating impact of World War 2, the atrocities committed by Nazi Germany in the name of racial supremacy, and the global wave of anti-colonialist sentiments that followed the peace settlement, that European nations began to find it politically impossible to continue to maintain their previous relations with South Africa. The break was, however, never final. The process of creeping sanctions, alienation and isolation imposed by European countries over an extended period sent a clear message though that the old epoch of special relations had come to an end and that their new commitment was to support majority rule in South Africa, irrespective of race, class or culture. When everything is taken into account, a significant share of both the blame and the praise for the good and the bad of South African development and history must be apportioned to the influence of European colonial rule and its political and economic practices.

Chapter 2
Europe and apartheid South Africa: The parting of ways

Introduction

After World War 2, South African/European relations assumed a dual character. Bilateral relations, dominated by the United Kingdom, Germany, France, Italy and the Netherlands, continued to exist, while relations with the European Community (EC) slowly took shape to become meaningful and substantial only after 1994. Special relations with the aforementioned countries were based on economic ties in particular, although the historical, cultural and sentimental relations that grew from centuries of European presence in South Africa and the latter's strategic importance to the West in the Cold War era also played a meaningful role. Because of the repugnance and global condemnation apartheid evoked, both bilateral relations with EC members and multilateral relations with the EC government in Brussels deteriorated sharply in the last quarter of the 20th century, with member countries like the Netherlands, Denmark and Ireland leading this cooler affiliation. It was, however, difficult to find absolute consensus on a common approach in the EC family: conservative administrations in the United Kingdom, Germany, France and Italy continued to maintain good working relations with Pretoria, mainly because of their dependence on the supply of strategic raw materials by the latter, trade, and the perceived geopolitical strategic value of South Africa during the Cold War. This attitudinal dichotomy was also reflected within the EC, where some nations applied sanctions with greater vigour and commitment than others. Although the EC kept Pretoria at arm's length from the start, it entered the active anti-apartheid campaign fairly late. Concrete action was only taken when South

Africa's pariah status in world politics was an indisputable reality, with the United Nations' (UN) sanctions regime already in place. The EC's sanctions policy came at a time when it was an unavoidable route to take, when there was no alternative but to follow world opinion as expressed in UN policies and actions.

Declining European influence in South Africa

After the demise of colonialism in the decade after World War 2 and with apartheid becoming the official political policy of the South African government in 1948, European influence declined while the country's international isolation increased. A policy that was regarded by the majority of whites as the road to permanent white security, privilege and hegemony turned out to be the way to catastrophe. Looking at the race policy of the National Party retrospectively, it is indeed hard to understand or explain the intellectual and moral cult as well as the profound ignorance that inspired and underpinned it. The policy of apartheid was an anachronism and a political paradox in the extreme. On the one hand, the Afrikaners' long and bloody struggle against British imperialism and the black indigenous population engendered a survival-at-all-cost national ethos, and the concentration of power at the exclusion of the majority of the population was an institutionalisation of the survival instinct. But on the other hand, what the Afrikaner supporters of the National Party did unto black South Africans was patently abominable, ignorant, short-sighted and inexcusable: theirs was a recipe that eventually resulted in permanent loss of power and marginalization for themselves, and pain, humiliation and hardship for the black population.

The victory of Afrikaner nationalism in 1948 and the hegemony that followed came at a time when historical forces began their inexorable move in a new direction, away from racism, colonialism and undemocratic rule. Apartheid was introduced immediately after the devastation of World War 2 and the costly eradication of European fascism, at a time when widespread and intense international repugnance and intolerance prevailed against any notion of racial superiority or racial discrimination. To add to the paradox, many South Africans fought on the side of the Allied forces against the Nazis during the war, and Field Marshall Jan Christiaan Smuts, an Afrikaner leader, played a pivotal role in the Allied command structure. Strongly under the influence of leaders who sympathized with the cause of Nazi Germany and who saw white supremacy as the only way to permanent political power, Afrikaner nationalism moved sharply to the extreme right of the political spectrum. Smuts was castigated as a sell-out to foreign interests and he and his party were pushed aside by the white voters in the 1948 election. Other factors that exacerbated the decline of South African relations with Europe were:

- Anti-British sentiment in the government and among its Afrikaner followers, mainly as a consequence of the Anglo-Boer War and the bitter memory of the grotesque atrocities of the British concentration camps
- South Africa's forced withdrawal from the Commonwealth after becoming a republic in 1961
- The mounting multilateral pressure applied by newly independent Third World governments as well as by national liberation movements such as the ANC and the UDF
- The spate of punitive sanctions imposed by the UN Security Council against South Africa at the insistence of mainly African and Asian states
- An increasingly hostile world public opinion against the policy of apartheid in South Africa, and the international sanctions and isolation that followed.

Bilateral European sanctions against South Africa

South African/European relations did not deteriorate immediately after 1948, but became progressively worse after decolonisation in Africa gained momentum and after a large number of newly independent Third World states became members of the United Nations, specialised agencies, the Organisation for African Unity (OAU), the Commonwealth and the Non-Aligned Movement (NAM). These organisations served as the main platform for a sustained international campaign against apartheid and the isolation of South Africa in the international arena. The EC and several of its member states (acting in their individual capacity) were not in the vanguard of this campaign, as was the case with the aforementioned organisations. Some member states did indeed follow stringent policies to isolate South Africa, but Community measures were generally ineffective while others preferred to follow the dictates of economic self-interest rather than moral duty.

Because foreign policy making in the Community is the sovereign domain of member states, the Commission in Brussels can only act after prior intergovernmental agreement. This lack of consensus and conflicting interests on the part of members are the main reasons why the EC entered the anti-apartheid scene so late and so uncoordinated. When EC punitive measures against South Africa were eventually instituted, they formed part of the worldwide campaign against apartheid, being preceded, influenced and dictated by the various compulsory UN Security Council decisions to persuade the South African government to end apartheid. As mentioned before, over and above the EC's overarching policy on sanctions, its member states followed their own preferences with respect to conducting bilateral relations with South Africa. Some opted for stringent measures, cutting all ties with the South African government, while others, acting out of self-interest, preferred to do the minimum. For a while South Africa's strong trade links with the United Kingdom, France, Germany, Belgium and Italy acted as a buffer against its full-scale isolation from Europe, although sanctions regimes imposed by the UN and later by the EC eventually forced these countries to downgrade and minimize their relationship with South Africa. Their response was to firstly apply selective and limited sanctions, acting strictly within the framework of compulsory sanctions approved by the UN Security Council.

Division in its own ranks was, therefore, an important reason for the slow and minimal Community response to join the anti-apartheid bandwagon. Voting on apartheid by member states of the United Nations up to the early 1980s reflected their different policies: on 70 anti-apartheid resolutions, the EC only voted together on 17 occasions.[1] So-called "essential interests", based on dependency on strategic raw materials from South Africa, kept the conservative administrations of particularly the United Kingdom, West Germany and France from following the example of principled sanctions supporters such as Denmark, the Netherlands and Ireland, whose dependency on South Africa's strategic raw materials was comparatively much smaller. Although an important mood change in British/South African relations set in after Prime Minister Harold Macmillan's "Winds of Change" speech in the South African Parliament in Cape Town on 3 February 1960, sanctions only followed much later. However, the Macmillan speech broke the ice as it were, and set both the tone and the new parameters for future relations, not only between South Africa and the United Kingdom, but also by implication other EC countries, who generally followed British leadership on the question of South Africa. This setback for South Africa's international position was further aggravated after the termination of its Commonwealth membership when it became a republic in

---

1 M. Holland, *The European Community and South Africa: European political cooperation under strain* (London, Pinter, 1988), pp. 61–72.

1961. Not being a member of the Commonwealth club any longer, South Africa became more vulnerable to the isolation drive of a growing number of critics. British censure of its domestic policies became more strident, isolation from Europe increased on a much broader front and stronger support was given to the Third World led sanctions campaign against the country.

Up to 1977, the European campaign was stronger in symbolism and rhetoric than in substance. South Africa's break with Europe was never total or final as some countries refrained from closing all channels of trade and diplomatic contact. Community sanctions were far from effective as "a web of loopholes through which trade and continued links with South Africa"[2] continued to exist for countries opposed to stringent measures. In many respects, therefore, the intensity of European states' fight against apartheid was lower than that of African, Scandinavian, Asian, Eastern European and Latin American countries and the Soviet Union. Throughout the apartheid years formal diplomatic ties were maintained between South Africa and most EC members (except Ireland, Denmark and Luxembourg). Trade continued to flow, with the exception of arms, Kruger rands and technological goods used to defend apartheid, which all fell under the UN sanctions regime. Less costly symbolic sanctions, particularly involving science, education, research, sport and culture were applied more rigorously as the international outcry against apartheid intensified after 1976. The EC and its member states could hardly afford to stay aloof or even ignore the increasingly angry international mood and tide of protest following the Soweto riots in 1976. The imposition of the UN mandatory arms embargo, the election of human rights activist Jimmy Carter as president of the United States of America and the impatience and animosity of newly independent African nations with the Pretoria regime made it simply incorrect and potentially embarrassing for Europe to be regarded as the odd man out. According to some observers, the Code of Conduct, which between 1977 and 1984 was the only instrument guiding the EC, "was designed to defend the European Governments from international criticism".[3]

The European Community's sanctions policy

At Community level, South Africa was essentially a low-priority issue until the United Kingdom joined the EC in 1973. Until 1977,

---

2 *Ibid.* p. 109.
3 Quoted in Holland, p. 33.

the EC generally followed the leadership of the United Kingdom. "Muddling through" under the United Kingdom's leadership, it was often "impossible to determine the exact nature of the goal or goals" sought by the Community.[4] Although the removal of apartheid and the economic liberation of Southern Africa were the overarching objectives sought by Brussels, its policies "lacked coherence" and "suffered from the ambiguous decisions taken".[5] On the whole, therefore, the EC's role to bring about change in South Africa was ineffective.

In 1976 the EC Council of Foreign Ministers issued its first declaration "condemning the policy of apartheid in South Africa". Eager to be seen at last as a serious participant in the international campaign against apartheid, the EC in 1977 adopted a voluntary "Code of Conduct" for European enterprises doing business in South Africa. This Code, a discredited and ineffective device, remained the flagship of EC anti-apartheid policy until the mid-1980s.[6] The main objective of the Code was to promote the working conditions for black workers of private entities in South Africa, covering aspects such as labour relations, wages, migrant labour, living standards and desegregation. Although it was Community policy, member states followed their own varying interpretations, with the result that the whole effort was by and large chaotic and badly implemented, monitored and administered. It generally had little to show in terms of achievement. What made this seem even worse was that until 1984, the Code was the only Community action aimed at ending apartheid.

In 1985 the deteriorating situation in South Africa motivated the EC to summon member states' ambassadors in South Africa to Europe for consultations. The decision was made to dispatch a Troika Diplomatic Mission (consisting of the foreign ministers of Luxembourg, Italy and the Netherlands) to South Africa. The Troika subsequently proposed to the Council of Foreign Ministers a broad range of restrictive measures against the government, but fell short of calling for economic sanctions. At the same time, the Troika proposed positive measures that would help the opponents of apartheid. The punitive measures included the withdrawal of military attachés, a ban on nuclear and military cooperation, a ban on new investments, a ban on oil sales and sensitive technology, the termination of official contacts and

---

4   D. Allen & P. Byrne, "Multilateral decision-making and implementation: The case of the European Community" in S. Smith & M. Clarke (eds), *Foreign policy implementation* (London, Allen & Unwin, 1985), p. 141.
5   Holland, pp. 95, 97.
6   *Ibid.* p. 37.

agreements on security, an embargo on exports of arms and paramilitary equipment, and a partial sport and cultural boycott. At the same time, it was proposed that non-violent anti-apartheid organisations should be financed, that assistance should be given to the educational needs of the non-white community, and that support should be given to the SADCC and the frontline states against South Africa's destabilization efforts in the region. From the start these restrictive measures were not unanimously accepted or uniformly interpreted and implemented by member states, but in the course of 1985 and 1986 they formed part of EC and member states' response to apartheid. In 1986 the EC's campaign against apartheid was intensified with the adoption of a partial ban on the importation of iron and steel from South Africa, a ban on new investments and the initiation of EC legislation on the ban of Kruger rands.[7]

The effectiveness of the EC and member states' restrictive measures aimed to end apartheid in South Africa was blunted by various factors such as internal divisions, different interpretations and emphases by member states, legal obscurities, ambiguities and ineffective implementation and administration. These actions also did not cut any ice with the ANC, the main liberation organisation, which preferred to remain aloof vis-à-vis the EC. When Sir Godfrey Howe visited South Africa in 1986 in his capacity as president of the EC Council of Foreign Ministers in an attempt to establish a policy framework for ending apartheid, Nelson Mandela and other ANC members refused to meet with him. The ANC response may have reflected doubt on its part on whether the EC's belated anti-apartheid action programme was an act of genuine compassion with the sufferers under the apartheid regime or an act of unavoidable necessity, political correctness and expediency. The gist of the ANC's response seems to be that the EC could have done more much sooner. Such a generalisation may appear to be unfair when bearing in mind what sort of organisation the EC is and the procedural and legal restrictions that complicated action against apartheid. Its pre-1994 policy towards South Africa also seems to be at variance with the constructive role it sought to play in the developing world since the adoption of the Treaties of Rome, particularly through the Yaoundé and Lomé Conventions with the ACP countries. Although South Africa was a former colony, a devel-

---

7   Holland, pp. 95–124; L. Fioramonti, "The European Union promoting democracy in South Africa: Strengths and weaknesses", unpublished paper delivered at Conference on the Relationship between Africa and the European Union, University of the Western Cape, 22–23 January 2004; J. Hanlon & R. Ormond, *The sanctions handbook* (Harmondsworth, Penguin, 1987), p. 172.

oping country and technically speaking a member of the ACP bloc, it was excluded from receiving EC development aid. This policy was in place before the anti-apartheid campaign appeared on the world agenda, and should be seen as a genuine response on the part of the EC to do something about the inequities and scars left by colonialism.

European Community assistance to the victims of apartheid

As pointed out, the EC's fairly belated actions against apartheid were mainly due to the reluctance of its larger members to adopt extreme policies.[8] However, once it was decided that a stricter approach should be adopted, an important pillar of South Africa's external relations crumbled. Europe was traditionally South Africa's cultural, intellectual and moral *heimat*, the land of the founding fathers, the main element of South Africa's diplomatic "inner circle", its biggest trading partner and its main foreign investor. Because of the sanctions regime, South Africa was effectively alienated and excluded from these roots. In more practical terms, the country was also denied access to the lucrative EC trade and development advantages that applied to former ACP colonies.

Before 1986, the EC role in the struggle against apartheid was limited to the usage of mainly verbal and symbolic instruments of diplomacy. Pretoria's diplomatic representation at the European Commission in Brussels remained in place while the EC withheld formal reciprocal diplomatic representation until after the collapse of apartheid and the election of a new democratic government in 1994. For the short period between 1991 and 1994, during the rule of the Government of National Unity (GNU), the EC maintained a Programme Coordination Office in Pretoria. Prior to 1991, the EC's posture of non-cooperation with the South African government was expressed in its decision to bar South Africa from EC-sponsored programmes, mainly the Lomé Accord with the ACP countries, and development aid and trade agreements. In response to the removal of apartheid and democratic change in South Africa, the EC started with a gradual process to lift sanctions.

Although the EC distanced itself progressively from the white minority government in South Africa from 1978, it also realized

---

8   See Holland, pp. 51–73; Fioramonti, "The European Union promoting democracy in South Africa", p. 4.

that for symbolic and humanitarian reasons it could not absolve itself totally from the South African situation and embarked on a "Special Programme" to "assist the victims of apartheid" (1986–1994). The programme, set out in an EC Foreign Ministers' statement on 10 September 1985, consisted of measures to:

- Assist non-violent anti-apartheid organisations, particularly the churches
- Assist the education of the non-white community, including grants for university studies
- Assist the SADCC and the frontline states
- Increase awareness among citizens of member states resident in South Africa
- Intensify contacts with the non-white community in a variety of sectors.

This programme for obvious reasons shunned any connection with the South African government of the time. Selected non-governmental organisations, mainly churches, the Kagiso Trust and the International Confederation of Free Trade Unions were used in an intermediary capacity. Between 1986 and 1994, ECU 450 million (approximately R2 billion), covering over 700 projects, was committed under the Special Programme. The programme, with an annual budget of ECU 125 million (about R800 million at 1998 rates, when the ECU was last used) in grants, was the largest single development programme in South Africa and the biggest of its kind implemented by the EC anywhere in the world. The main focus of the aid and development programmes was to support peaceful change and development in the fields of education and training, humanitarian and social aid, health and welfare, rural and agricultural development, community building, good governance, job creation and legal assistance. All these programmes were expected to subscribe and promote peaceful transition, non-racialism, democracy and the "people-driven development principle" in one way or another. This programme helped a great deal to restore the EC's image among black South Africans.

Positive political reforms in South Africa also motivated the EC to lift sanctions, albeit gradually. In February 1991, the EC's investment ban was abandoned and in 1992, several other sanctions were dispensed with. Military sanctions were only lifted on 27 May 1994. Following the democratic elections in South Africa and the formation of the GNU in 1994, the EU's role in development cooperation in South Africa increased substantially. The European Programme for Reconstruction and Development (EPRD) in South Africa superseded the Special Programme, with the specific aim of supporting the GNU's Reconstruction and Development Programme (RDP).

At the outset, these lavishly funded EC programmes (after November 1993, the EC became the EU) were applied rather randomly and without a clear developmental focus. The widespread euphoria following South Africa's miraculous peaceful transformation from apartheid to non-racial democracy seemed to have momentarily influenced Brussels to abandon its traditionally rigid Official Development Assistance (ODA) criteria and to rush headlong into financing a plethora of projects in South Africa. In 1994 alone, over 50 projects at an average of ECU 2 million per project were approved. However, in 1995, greater circumspection set in and the number was reduced to ten in order to make the effort more focused and manageable. Greater thrust and focus also followed from the signing of the "Declaration of Intent" between South Africa and the EU in 1995, the development of a "Country Strategy Paper" in 1996, and the approval of a new legal basis for development and cooperation with South Africa by the EU Council of Ministers on 22 November 1996. South Africa and the EU Commission also reached an agreement towards the end of 1996 to cooperate in the field of science and technology, with the aim of redressing imbalances caused by apartheid and sanctions. The agreement further intended to improve the competitiveness of the South African economy in the global economy and to promote the advantages of the information technology in the country.

Conclusion

Initially, the minimal contact between South Africa and the EC was due to a lack of interest as well as general dissatisfaction with the race policies of the Pretoria government. The slow EC reaction and the insignificance of its early actions indicated apathy to the aberrations of apartheid. Engagement only followed when it was no longer possible to hide behind inadequate half-measures. The sanctions regime the EC eventually agreed on in the mid-1980s made a strong impact on the South African situation, and the fact that this was balanced by a substantial aid programme for the victims of apartheid was an indication of the type of role the EC could play when fully committed. Full and normal relations with the EC were only established after the final demise of apartheid in 1994. At that time, the EU (formerly the EC) had established itself as a major international economic role player, while South Africa entered the world stage basking in the glow of its much-heralded peaceful and democratic transformation. Presently, South Africa again enjoys beneficial bilateral relations with all its traditional partners in Western Europe, as well as with the rest of Europe. With its relations with the EU also on a normal footing, Europe has unquestionably become a main pillar of South African foreign relations, particularly from an economic and commercial point of view.

Chapter 3
South Africa's foreign policy and national interests in the context of the EU's international role

Introduction

In various ways, the European Union/South African relationship is unique when compared to the latter's bilateral relations with state actors. With its being a multilateral organisation with a limited foreign policy mandate, the EU seems to be regarded in the South African public eye as something like a Good Samaritan, an amorphous entity, without the gravitas and diplomatic authority of a major power. Although a more sophisticated view exists at official level, the EU is not among South Africa's closest worldly relations. The important and substantial contribution it makes to South Africa's welfare and security does not translate into the political/diplomatic influence one would have expected. This seems to be due to both ideology and the EU's status as a global political role player.

Economic giant but political dwarf

For most of its existence, the EU has maintained external relations with non-member countries. These relations used to be basically non-political and concentrated mainly on common trade affairs and development aid to developing countries in the Southern hemisphere. Over the years, a great deal of substance was added to this role, although it has remained largely apolitical. As a result the EU's relevance in world affairs has continued to be a derivative of its economic power. It has given priority to promoting trade and development and has played an increasingly prominent role in currently salient international issues like trade liberalization, world poverty, human rights, conflict resolution, sustainable development, environmental issues and problems, and globalisation issues. Its autonomous commercial policy has covered all the measures taken outside the scope of treaty obligations with non-member countries regarding imports and exports. These have included tariff structures, anti-dumping measures, unfair trade practices by third countries or illicit trade practices, measures against subsidized imports, quotas and trade bans (sanctions or embargoes) as well as its unfair and protectionist Common Agricultural Policy (CAP).

South Africa's relations with the EU do not reflect the same substance and attitudinal nuances as is the case with its relations with the other major powers. This has much to do with the EU's multilateral character, its pluralistic approach to international security and foreign policy matters, its reliance on "soft power", its muted political role in the global political arena beyond the boundaries of Europe, and its generally low-risk diplomacy. As stated by McCormick: "The world does not know what to make of the European Union, in large part because the European Union does not yet quite know what to make of itself. The core problem is one of definition: The EU is neither a state nor a super state, and yet it is much more than a conventional international organization".[1] A Belgian foreign minister depicted it metaphorically as "an economic giant, a political dwarf and a military worm".[2]

In spite of the EU's considerable latent power, it punches far below its weight in global politics and plays second fiddle to the major powers of the world in the big issues of the day, except in world trade matters and development aid. These aspects have been assigned to the Commission, which makes policy on behalf of the member states. The EU's lack of political and military clout is obviously an anomaly, bearing in mind the impressive quantitative aspects of the EU's power base. According to Javier Solana: "As a union of 25 states with over 450 million people producing a quarter of the world's Gross National Product (GNP), and with a wide range of instruments to its disposal, the European Union is inevitably a global player".[3] Even before the 2004 enlargement, the EU accounted for one-fifth of global trade, although its then 15 members represented only 6% of the world population. Its share of world merchandise trade (intra-EU excluded) was 19.2%

---

1 J. McCormick, *Understanding the European Union: A concise introduction* (London, Macmillan, 1999), p. 202.
2 Quoted in McCormick, p. 206.
3 J. Solana, *A secure Europe in a better world: European Security Strategy* (Paris, The European Union Institute for Security Studies, 2002), p. 4.

(US 18.1%), and its share of world trade in commercial services (intra-EU excluded) was 26.1% (US 23.2%).⁴ In short, the EU is the world's biggest market place. Obviously it will have more global influence if member states acted as a group rather than independently in matters of foreign policy and security. A dilemma yet to have been overcome is how to deal with matters of general European interest without interfering with the right of members to conduct their own sovereign affairs.

As a global economic giant, the EU wields considerable power in areas such as international trade, development aid, economy, monetary matters, science and technology. Although it works with one arm tied behind its back on most foreign policy issues, it has recently emerged as a prominent role player in maintaining pan-European security, combating international terrorism, stopping the clandestine spread of weapons of mass destruction (specifically nuclear arms), policing drug trafficking and settling regional conflicts.⁵ An outstanding testimony of the EU's successful use of soft power is its recent achievements in affecting constructive political changes in the Ukraine, Turkey and Bosnia. According to one observer, the EU "does not change countries by threatening them. Its biggest threat is not intervention but withdrawal of the hand of friendship and especially the prospect of membership".⁶ Even so, outside its European sphere of influence, the EU's political role is much inferior to that of the United States, the only super power of this era. The multilateralism it represents is obviously an inferior power in an essentially bipolar world. In ACP countries where the EU made huge investments in terms of ODA and trade deals, its influence is low and disproportionate to its inputs, while in regions like Latin America, Central Asia and the Far East its role is muted and ineffectual.

The tussle between federalism (supranationalism) and confederalism (intergovernmentalism) as models of European Union integration

There is a prominent school of thought that believes that the preferable and most effective future role of the EU in world affairs would be to work from a multilateral platform to establish

---

4 European Commission, "The European Union and world trade" (Brussels, Directorate-general for Information, Communication, Culture and Audio-visual Publications Unit, 1999), pp. 3–4.
5 Solana, *A secure Europe in a better world*, pp. 10–14.
6 M. Leonard, "Why the US needs the EU", *Time*, 28 February 2005, p. 27.

BOX 2 ESSENTIAL STRUCTURAL AND FUNCTIONAL CHARACTERISTICS OF THE EUROPEAN UNION

The term European Union (EU) refers to the 25 European states currently integrated into a pluralistic community for the achievement of common economic, social, political and security goals. Member states by mutual agreement pool their sovereignty in specified areas of shared regional cooperation. Institutionally and functionally, the EU reflects a complicated mixture of supranationalism (federalism and functionalism) and intergovernmentalism (confederalism). Policy decisions are made by way of a complex, if not arcane interaction between the main institutions of the EU: the European Council (heads of government and the EU president), the Council of Foreign Ministers (ministers of member states), the elected European Parliament, the European Commission and the EU Court of Justice. The 25 member European Commission, appointed by the member states' national governments for five years, is seated in Brussels. Once appointed, commissioners swear an oath of office renouncing loyalty to the national interests of the respective countries they come from. The Commission, acting on the basis of joint responsibility, is the main initiator of EU laws and policies and also functions as the main administrative organ of the EU. The dominant figure in the Commission is the president, appointed by the member states for renewable five-year terms. For all practical purposes the president must be regarded as the leader of the EU. The Council of Ministers, representing member states and assisted by the Committee of Permanent Representatives (Coreper), makes final decisions on proposals by the Commission, in conjunction with the European Parliament. A country holds the presidency of the Council of Ministers and of the European Council for six months. The popularly elected 786 member European Parliament represents the interests of EU citizens, and the European Court of Justice ensures conformity to national and EU laws with treaties. A European Union, founded on the existing three European Communities, was created with the conclusion in November 1993 of the Treaty of the European Union (commonly known as the Maastricht Treaty). Reflecting its hybrid character, the European Union consists of three main pillars: European Community, Common Foreign and Security Policy, and Home Affairs and Justice.

a global sphere of influence through trade, finance, and foreign investment.[7] The European Security Strategy (ESS) adopted by the European Council in December 2003, which stated that the EU would seek an international order based on effective multilateralism, confirmed this view.[8] This school rejects a polar type power-political role for the EU, backed by military power similar to that of a conventional major world power.[9] Like former United States president, Woodrow Wilson, at the end of World War 1, they believe that peace could be fostered by "the removal, as far as possible, of all economic barriers and the establishment of equality of trade conditions among all nations consenting to the peace and associating themselves for its maintenance".[10] This way of thinking challenges the ruling state-centric orthodoxy and presents a clash of paradigms: the realist Westphalian paradigm versus the liberal Wilsonian paradigm. While the Commission in Brussels practices multilateralism, some individual member states remain firm disciples of the intergovernmental paradigm. In 2005 this was largely confirmed by the negative reaction in the United Kingdom, France and the Netherlands to the new proposed federal-type of constitution, resulting in much loss of prestige and momentum to the organisation.

Of course, the reality is that the sovereignty based Westphalian state system still dominates the global political process, giving the advantage to the major powers and undercutting the role of multilateral organisations such as the UN and the EU. The question is, therefore, how the EU can assert itself with its not being a member of the UN Security Council or the G8, with NATO still entrusted with the security of Europe, and with its not being able to compete with the major powers in determining the international political agenda. The former president of the EU, Romano Prodi, envisaged a more prominent political role for the organisation: "If we want to satisfy the rising expectations and hopes of countries abroad and the peoples of Europe, we have to become a real global player".[11] Federalists in the EU fraternity share the same view. If the new recommendations of the constitutional European Convention under the chairmanship of former French president, Valéry Giscard d'Estaing, are realized, this could become part of the future scenario. The Draft Con-

---

7 Ibid.
8 M. Ortega, "Global views on the European Union", Challiot Paper, no. 72 (November 2004), p. 117.
9 Ibid. pp. 125–128.
10 C. W. Kegley (ed.), Controversies in international relations theory: Realism and the neo-liberal challenge (New York, St Martins, 1995), p. 13.
11 R. Prodi, "A wider Europe: A proximity policy as the key to stability", speech at the Sixth ECSA-World Conference, Brussels, 5–6 December 2002.

stitutional Treaty (Articles 1–3 and III–292) expands on the ESS formulation:

> The union's action on the international scene shall be guided by, and designed to advance in the wider world, the principles which have inspired its own creation, development and enlargement: democracy, the rule of law, the universality and indivisibility of human rights and fundamental freedoms, respect for human rights, the principles of equality and solidarity, and respect for the principles of the United Nations Charter and international law. The Union shall seek to develop relations and build partnerships with third countries, and international, regional or global organisations that share the principles referred to in the first subparagraph. It shall promote multilateral solutions to common problems, in particular in the framework of the United Nations.

According to Martin Ortega, this description of the EU's international role does not offend any of the world powers: "no state or international actor perceives the European Union as a strategic threat, because it represents a new approach to global politics".[12] However, laudable as these ideals might be, they seem to underestimate the pervasive role of national based power politics in the world at large. As the United Nations has regularly experienced in the past, multilateralism must invariably bow to orthodox sovereign state power when the latter's national interests come into play. It seems, therefore, a well-nigh impossible challenge for the EU to replace the conventional Westphalian paradigm, which continues to dominate world politics, with a system based on multilateralism. From a normative, teleological perspective the liberal EU multilateral paradigm is undoubtedly the better model for the future of world affairs, but it will probably remain a utopian aspiration for decades to come. Presently the power of the United States goes virtually unchallenged and with countries like China, India, Japan and Russia moving up the world power hierarchy, multilateralism will remain a secondary force. If the EU were to develop into a "a kind of United States of Europe" as Winston Churchill had envisaged in 1946[13] and present a united front, its multilateral status could be transformed into a more meaningful role as a global player powerful enough to exercise a countervailing influence in the global distribution of power.

---

12 Ortega, p. 119.
13 W. S. Churchill, "The tragedy of Europe", quoted in B. F. Nelsen & A. C-G. Stubb (eds), *The European Union: Readings on the theory and practice of European integration* (London, Lynne Rienner, 1998), p. 8.

The EU can only blame itself for its ineffectiveness as a global political force. It seems perennially stuck while vacillating between the Scylla and Charybdis of supranationalism and statecentrism. And it seems prepared to muddle through indefinitely.

The rejection of the new Constitutional Treaty by French and Dutch voters in May 2005, the United Kingdom's decision to defer a referendum on the Treaty, and the EC's subsequent decision to postpone the November 2006 deadline (by which all members were to have ratified the new Constitutional Treaty), point to a victory of confederalism over federalism. As such it is also a victory for the status quo. What is therefore likely to emerge in future years is more intergovernmentalism and less supranationalism in the way Europe is governed. If this is the case, Brussels' efforts to assure a greater global role for the EU are likely to founder. In practice this means that the EU will not empower itself sufficiently to act with greater impact, authority and legitimacy in world politics. The imperfect contemporary world political system will endure and the EU's role in dealing with pressing post-Cold War, post-Saddam Hussein, and post-September 11 realities will remain limited. Moreover, the debilitating cleavages between Europe and the United States, and among European states themselves, affected by the catastrophic Iraq crisis, will probably linger on as Europe takes a step back in history to once again and with renewed enthusiasm embrace the false promises and dangerous lure of the statecentrism of old Westphalian Europe.

European Union lack of foreign policy unity means lack of power and influence

If the EU was to emerge as a stronger, more influential and assertive factor in world politics, South Africa and other countries' policy makers would be forced to re-evaluate the organisation as an authority in the country's national interests. But under prevailing circumstances there is no urgent need to do so. From a North-South perspective and given the EU's long track record in the development field, and particularly its generally sympathetic stance vis-à-vis the developing world, a stronger political influence in world politics could have helped a great deal to influence the debate between North and South and to restore better understanding and greater global equity. Today we have the utterly contradictory situation where the United Kingdom unilaterally promotes an African debt relieve and aid plan on its own, while it is an EU member as well as a signatory member of the Cotonou Agreement. Of course, expedient solo efforts such

TABLE 1 MEMBERS OF THE EUROPEAN UNION (2004)

	Population (million)	Land area (km²)	GDP (€ billion)	Date of accession
France	57	544 000	1557	1957
West Germany*				1957
Belgium	10	30 519	267	1957
Netherlands	15	41 526	453	1957
Luxembourg	0.4	2586	24	1957
Italy	9.6	301 263	1301	1957
Denmark	5.2	43 080	188	1973
Ireland	4	93 036	132	1973
UK	60.3	252 000	1589	1973
Greece	10.6	131 940	153	1981
Portugal	10.3	92 102	130	1986
Spain	40.8	504 800	743	1986
Germany	82.5	357 021	2129	1990
Austria	7.8	83 857	224	1995
Finland	5.1	338 000	143	1995
Sweden	8.8	450 000	267	1995
Hungary	10.2	93 036	73	2004
Slovakia	5.4	49 035	28	2004
Czech Republic	10.3	79 000	76	2004
Slovenia	2	20 000	24	2004
Poland	36.8	312 685	185	2004
Malta	0.4	316	14	2004
Cyprus	0.8	9250	11	2004
Lithuania	3.6	65 000	16	2004
Estonia	1.4	45 227	24.5	2004
Latvia	2.3	64 000	9	2004

*See Germany.

as these to boost the national prestige are not novel or strange among EU member states, the majority of whom promote their own ODA programmes, in effect duplicating EU efforts. These developments do nothing but reinforce the maladies of the prevailing *pax Americana*, which has not made the world a better place for either the developing nations or Europe. The present United States administration prefers to deal with a divided Europe, and the same could probably be said about the United Kingdom. A strong and united EU voice at G8 meetings where

Map of the European Union[14]

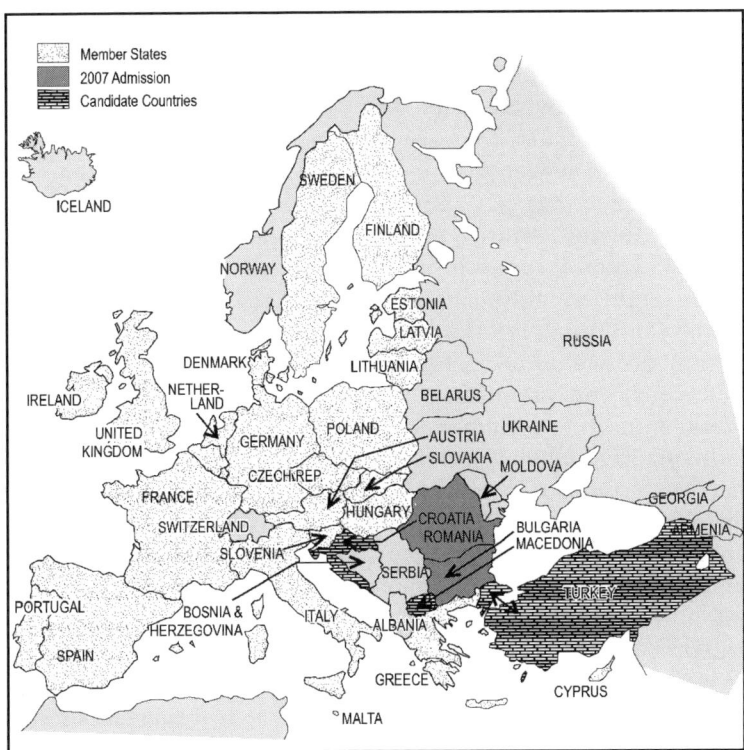

the African poverty dilemma is discussed would undoubtedly be advantageous to the developing world. Even taking into account that "enlightened" self-interest lies close to the heart of EU trade and aid practices and that more political power would not necessarily translate into greater benevolence or altruism towards developing nations, the checks and balances of a multipolar configuration, preferably based on multilateralism, would undoubtedly make the world a safer place and alleviate the plight of underdeveloped nations of the Southern hemisphere.

Conclusion

An interesting paradox in the debate about the plight of the developing world is that greater saliency does not translate into

---

14 Wikipedia, "Image. EU map", 2006, <http://en.wikipedia.org/wik/Image: EU_map_names_isles.png>.

greater progress in dealing with this matter. Although the developing nations must share a large portion of the blame for the state they are in, much of the problem also lies with the industrialised nations in the G8 who monopolise the agenda of development aid and poverty relief. The G8 busy themselves with the Third World because they are in a position to do so due to their resources and power, they feel obliged to do it because there is an expectation that they should play a role, and they feel attracted to the theme because it brings global prestige and recognition. Even so, when it comes to the practical side of things, the state-centric approach automatically relegates assistance to the developing world to an inferior position in relation to national interests. Hence we do not get much beyond periodical aspirational statements and promises. A remedy could be to assign Third World support to supranational role players like the EU, but the industrialised nations do not even consider this possibility. They need not consider it, as the EU itself is a house divided with development assistance being given by both the Commission and the member states. In South Africa too the role of the EU is diluted by the fact that its member states follow their own interests and run their own development programmes. The situation will probably not change in the foreseeable future in view of current policies and preferences in Europe. This is a pity seeing as the EU is potentially in the best position to bring about the changes needed to transform the world.

Chapter 4
The evolution of the European Union's development policy

Introduction

Since the mid-1970s the EU has increasingly been involved in development policy. In the absence of clearly defined powers, it has gradually developed its own policy instruments and a financial framework in harmony with the operational codes of its member states. It had, however, no development powers of its own. The Maastricht Treaty on European Union, initially approved in December 1991, gave a clearer definition of EU responsibilities to complement the activities of member states. In spite of the lack of formal powers, the EU developed a wide range of activities in the field of North-South cooperation. Cooperation under the Lomé Conventions (1970–2000) and their successor, the Cotonou Agreement, lies at the heart of the Community development policy.

Aims and objectives of European Union development policy

The Maastricht Treaty of 1992 (Title XVII) and the Amsterdam Treaty (Title XX) strengthened the legal base for the Community's development policy. Development cooperation is a shared competence of the EU and its member states. EU development policy, according to Articles 177 to 181 of the Treaty of the EU, will be complementary to the policies pursued by the member states. The general aims have been set out as fostering:
- The sustainable economic and social development of the developing countries, and more particularly the most disadvantaged among them

- The smooth and gradual integration of the developing countries into the world economy
- The campaign against poverty in the developing countries
- The development and consolidation of democracy, the rule of law and respect for human rights and fundamental freedoms.¹

At the time of its inception, the present EU (then going under the name of the EEC) was a small six-member organisation and its venture into development assistance was mostly about the promotion of trade, agricultural interests and development. The ACP states were secure and cheap suppliers of key raw materials and a captive future market for European exports of manufactured goods.

Through the years, the EU aid programmes were justified and articulated in broadly idealistic, altruistic and humanitarian terms. In 1982, the "Pisani Memorandum" defined the objectives concerning support for developing countries under the general heading of promotion of "peace throughout the world" and prioritised six practical aims:
- Support for developing countries' own efforts
- Promotion of self-sufficiency in food with emphasis on agricultural development
- Development of human resources
- Development of independent capabilities in scientific and applied research
- Systematic use of all available natural resources
- Restoration and maintenance of the ecological balance.²

From Yaoundé to Lomé to Cotonou

The EU development policy went through various phases, punctuated by the Yaoundé Conventions (1963–1974), the four Lomé Conventions (1975–2000) and the present ACP/EU Partnership Agreement, commonly known as the Cotonou Agreement (2000–). Yaoundé focussed mainly on former French and Belgian colonies in Africa. Largely due to the United Kingdom's membership of the EC, the Lomé Conventions superseded Yaoundé in 1975 to incorporate former British colonies. The EU has been a party to international food agreements since 1969. Since 1971 it

---

1 W. Weidenfeld & W. Wessels, *Europe from A to Z: Guide to European integration* (Luxemburg, Institut für Europäische Politik, 1997), p. 69.
2 *Ibid.*

has granted developing countries unilateral trade benefits under its generalized system of preferences; from the mid-1970s it has provided financial and emergency aid to ACP countries.[3] The fourth Lomé Convention also concerned itself with the question of ACP indebtedness, environmental protection and human rights.

The first Lomé Convention was concluded in 1975 between the EEC and 46 ACP states. The number of ACP participants grew to 77 (48 African, 15 Caribbean, 14 Pacific) by the conclusion of the fourth Convention in 1990. Lomé provided for trade cooperation, a stabilisation of export earnings regimes (STABEX (System of Stabilisation of Export Earnings) and SYSMIN (System to Stabilize ACP Countries' Earnings from Mining)), a sugar protocol and technical and financial cooperation:

- Trade and aid were the main instruments of Lomé. It granted ACP countries associated status with the EU, offering their products 99% duty free entry into the EU market as well as ODA. However, less than 1% of ACP agricultural products were covered by the deal (the rest being proscribed by the EU's Common Agricultural Policy), while 95% of EU imports from the ACP were primary products.
- STABEX provided a cushion to protect and stabilise export earnings in times of dramatic price fluctuations.
- SYSMIN was similar to STABEX, but applied only to countries dependent on specific mineral exports, responsible for at least 15% of export earnings over four years.
- The sugar protocol committed the EU to buy specific quantities of cane sugar from ACP countries at guaranteed prices.
- Technical and financial cooperation to assist rural development were financed by the European Development Fund (EDF) and the European Investment Bank (EIB).

However, the results of Lomé were disappointing as the ACP share of EU trade declined steadily over the years (by about 3% between 1975 and 1990).[4] In response to the new post-Cold War circumstances, particularly the enlargement of the EU, changes in the global trading system, trade liberalisation and the globalisation of the EU's development policy to include non-ACP countries, the unsatisfactory results of Lomé and the increasing international saliency of the Third World poverty syndrome, a new ODA approach became imperative. While under Lomé, the EU

---
3 *Ibid.* pp. 67–70.
4 *Ibid.* p. 70.

regarded barrier-free international trade and development incentives as the main locomotive of change in developing countries. The new Cotonou Partnership Agreement narrowed the focus to the central objective to "reduce and eventually eradicate poverty while contributing to sustainable development and to the gradual integration of the ACP countries into the world economy".[5]

To this end, Cotonou concentrated on five interrelated themes:
- The political dimension (political dialogue)
- Economic partnership and participation (involving state and non-state actors)
- Trade based on non-reciprocal preferences to be followed (in 2008) by a set of Economic Partnership Agreements (EPAs)
- Aid (financial and technical cooperation)
- Regionalization.

As it was clear that sustained development required an interdisciplinary and integrated approach, Cotonou sought to strike a balance between aid and trade on the one hand and on the other the moral, democratic and political, including poverty reduction and good governance. The introduction of a political dimension paved the way for the implementation of "political conditionalities", which meant in effect imposing certain standards regarding political liberalization and good governance that receivers of EU development assistance had to adhere to.[6]

It is important to note that the EU initially wanted a stronger political foundation to Cotonou. It wanted to include good governance as an "essential element", the violation of which could lead to a suspension of EU aid. However, it ultimately caved in to ACP demands and settled for the term "fundamental element", meaning that a lack of good governance would not constitute grounds for suspension.

Like Lomé, Cotonou is an ambitious plan to help the ACP states to overcome their underdeveloped status. It took a quarter of a century for the EU to conclude that Lomé was not the answer to the problems faced by the ACP states. It remains to be seen whether Cotonou will do better. The main objectives and

---

5 Cotonou Infokit, "The Cotonou Agreement at a glance (2)", (ECDPM 2001) <http;//www.one world.org/ecdpm/en/Cotonou_gb.htm>, (p. 1), Maastricht, ECDPM.
6 *ACP/EU Courier*, Special Issue: Cotonou Agreement (September 2000), pp. 6–10.

TABLE 2 THE AFRICAN, CARIBBEAN AND PACIFIC COUNTRIES

	Country	Capital	Area (km²)	Population (2003 estimate)
1	Angola	Luanda	1 246 700	10 766 471
2	Antigua and Barbuda	Saint John's	443	67 897
3	Bahamas, The	Nassau	13 940	297 477
4	Barbados	Bridgetown	431	277 264
5	Belize	Belmopan	22 966	266 440
6	Benin	Porto-Novo	112 620	7 041 490
7	Botswana	Gaborone	600 370	1 573 267
8	Burkina Faso	Ouagadougou	274 200	13 228 460
9	Burundi	Bujumbura	27 830	6 096 156
10	Cameroon	Yaoundé	475 440	15 746 179
11	Cape Verde	Praia	4033	412 137
12	Central African Republic	Bangui	622 984	3 683 538
13	Chad	N'Djamena	1 284 000	9 253 493
14	Comoros	Moroni	2170	632 948
15	Congo, Democratic Republic of the	Kinshasa	2 345 410	6 625 039
16	Congo, Republic of the	Brazzaville	342 000	2 954 258
17	Cook Islands	Avarua	240	21 008
18	Côte d'Ivoire	Yamoussoukro	322 460	16 962 491
19	Cuba	Havana	110 860	11 263 429
20	Djibouti	Djibouti	23 000	457 130
21	Dominica	Roseau	754	69 655
22	Dominican Republic	Santo Domingo	48 730	8 715 602
23	East Timor	Dili	15 007	997 853
24	Equatorial Guinea	Malabo	28 051	510 473
25	Eritrea	Asmara	121 320	4 362 254
26	Ethiopia	Addis Ababa	1 127 127	66 557 553
27	Fiji	Suva	18 270	868 531
28	Gabon	Libreville	267 667	1 321 560
29	Gambia, The	Banjul	11 300	1 501 050
30	Ghana	Accra	239 460	20 467 747
31	Grenada	Saint George's	344	89 258
32	Guinea	Conakry	245 857	9 030 220
33	Guinea-Bissau	Bissau	36 120	1 360 827
34	Guyana	Georgetown	214 970	702 100
35	Haiti	Port-au-Prince	27 750	7 527 817
36	Jamaica	Kingston	10 991	2 695 867
37	Kenya	Nairobi	582 650	31 639 091
38	Kiribati	Tarawa	811	98 549
39	Lesotho	Maseru	30 355	1 861 959
40	Liberia	Monrovia	111 370	3 317 176
41	Madagascar	Antananarivo	587 040	16 979 744
42	Malawi	Lilongwe	118 480	11 651 239
43	Mali	Bamako	1 240 000	11 626 219

	Country	Capital	Area (km²)	Population (2003 estimate)
44	Marshall Islands	Majuro	181	56 429
45	Mauritania	Nouakchott	1 030 700	2 912 584
46	Mauritius	Port Louis	2040	1 210 447
47	Micronesia, Federated States of	Palikir	702	108 143
48	Mozambique	Maputo	801 590	17 479 266
49	Namibia	Windhoek	825 418	1 927 447
50	Nauru	No official capital	21	12 570
51	Niger	Niamey	1 267 000	11 058 590
52	Nigeria	Abuja	923 768	133 881 703
53	Niue	Alofi	260	2145
54	Palau	Koror	458	19 717
55	Papua New Guinea	Port Moresby	462 840	5 295 816
56	Rwanda	Kigali	26 338	7 810 056
57	Saint Kitts and Nevis	Basseterre	261	38 763
58	Saint Lucia	Castries	616	162 157
59	Saint Vincent and the Grenadines	Kingstown	389	116 812
60	Samoa	Apia	2944	178 173
61	São Tomé and Príncipe	São Tomé	1001	175 883
62	Senegal	Dakar	196 190	10 580 307
63	Seychelles	Victoria	455	80 469
64	Sierra Leone	Freetown	71 740	5 732 681
65	Solomon Islands	Honiara	28 450	509 190
66	Somalia	Mogadishu	637 657	8 025 190
67	South Africa	Pretoria*	1 219 912	42 768 678
68	Sudan	Khartoum	2 505 810	38 114 160
69	Suriname	Paramaribo	163 270	435 449
70	Swaziland	Mbabane†	17 363	1 161 219
71	Tanzania	Dar es Salaam	945 087	35 922 454
72	Togo	Lomé	56 785	5 429 299
73	Tonga	Nuku'alofa	748	108 141
74	Trinidad and Tobago	Port-of-Spain	5128	1 104 209
75	Tuvalu	Fongafale	26	11 305
76	Uganda	Kampala	236 040	25 632 794
77	Vanuatu	Port-Vila	12 200	199 414
78	Zambia	Lusaka	752 614	10 307 333
79	Zimbabwe	Harare	390 580	12 576 742
			25 503 103	742 724 651
	World		510 072 000	6 302 309 691
			5%	12%

Source: *The World Factbook 2002* and *The World Factbook 2003*
*Pretoria is the administrative capital, Cape Town the legislative capital, and Bloemfontein the judicial capital.
†Mbabane is the administrative capital and Lobamba is the royal and legislative capital.

BOX 3 ECONOMIC PARTNERSHIP AGREEMENTS UNDER COTONOU AGREEMENT[7]

Economic Partnership Agreements (EPAs) under Cotonou Agreement (to be negotiated between 2002 and 2008) will include:
- Enhanced market access to the EU, which includes looking at remaining tariffs, non-tariff barriers and rules of origin
- A gradual and managed liberalisation of African economies, accompanied by the necessary support measures
- Increased cooperation in trade related areas like competition and investment
- A deepening of the regional integration process in Africa
- A flexible approach on trade in services
- A close link between development cooperation and trade
- EPAs will offer sub-Saharan Africa and the EU a fully WTO-compatible and open trade regime from 2008 onwards.

principles of Cotonou, i.e. equal partnership and ownership, participation, political dialogue and regional differentiation, seem to address some previous deficiencies and may make the necessary difference. Liberal funding is also available (around €25.2 billion through the EDF for the first five-year period). But effective implementation and producing visible results will be the real test. At first glance, Cotonou comes across equally Byzantine as Lomé. While it may be something of a bureaucratic masterpiece, the question is whether ordinary people in the ACP countries would ever be able to participate in any meaningful way in something they do not completely comprehend. Pressures for change in the EU development policy emanating from both inside and outside the EU are on the increase. According to various official reports, it has had various flaws:[8]
- It is too fragmented and complex. Changes in the functional scope of EU aid programmes were not accompanied by adaptive measures in the Commission, leading to serious flaws in the management and implementation of these programmes.

---
7 *Ibid.*
8 See R. A. Jones, *The politics and economics of the European Union: An introductory text*, 2nd edn (Cheltenham, Edward Elgar, 2001), p. 426.

- Inadequate staffing. The Commission failed to match staffing levels to aid volumes and to the increasing complexity of its aid portfolio.
- Sluggish and unresponsive delivery. There have been long delays in delivering aid projects, including a backlog of unfinished projects. By 2000 the EU had about €20 billion in unpaid commitments and a backlog of 1200 projects.
- Inadequate monitoring and financial control of projects. Too many control authorities lead to confusion and duplication.
- Lack of coherence. Development policies and other EU policies, particularly trade and environment, are not properly attuned to each other.
- Poor targeting. Aid has been spread too thinly on too many projects.
- Poor coordination. EU aid programmes and member states' bilateral programmes are not orchestrated properly, resulting in waste, confusion and duplication.

According to an OECD peer review of the EU development assistance: "There is no coherent Commission-wide development strategy or statement on development cooperation and the policies on country macro-economic and sector approaches, project and programme identification, implementation, procurement and evaluation lack Commission-wide consistency and coherence."[9] Equally important is the development of a definition of poverty and, following from this, a common EU understanding and interpretation of poverty. According to a 1999 study: "The crude benchmark of absolute poverty of a dollar a day is a useful but rather limited tool. Poverty measurement must take into account social indicators such as education, health, and access to services and infrastructure. Moreover, less tangible aspects also need to be covered such as livelihood insecurity, social exclusion, absence of choice and powerlessness. Unless the EU defines the problem in all its complexity, 'solutions' can at best be of limited value".[10] The same could be said about the EU's vagueness about what constitutes "good governance" in ACP countries. Without clarity on these development problems and issues, and without a strict application regime, Cotonou may end up with the same unconvincing track record as Lomé before it.

---

9 Towards True Partnership: EU-Africa Summit – A CIDSE Position Paper <http://www.cidse.org/pubs/euafpt2.htm>, p. 1.
10 Ibid.

BOX 4 FUNDAMENTAL PRINCIPLES OF THE COTONOU AGREEMENT[11]

- Equality of partners and ownership of the development strategies: for the purposes of implementing the objectives of partnership, the ACP states shall determine the development strategies for their economies and societies in all sovereignty.
- Respect for human rights and fundamental freedoms: these are an integral part of sustainable development, respect for fundamental social rights, democracy based on the rule of law and transparent and accountable governance.
- Participation: apart from the central government as the main partner, the partnership shall be open to different kinds of other actors in order to encourage the integration of all sectors of society, including the private sector and civil society organisations, into the mainstream of political, economic and social life.
- The pivotal role of dialogue and the fulfilment of mutual obligations: the obligations assumed by the Parties in the framework of their dialogue shall be central to their partnership and cooperation relations.
- Differentiation and regionalization: cooperation arrangements and priorities shall vary according to a partner's level of development, its needs, its performance and its long-term development strategy. Particular emphasis shall be placed on the regional dimension. Special treatment shall be given to the least developed countries. The vulnerability of landlocked and island countries shall be taken into account.

European Union development policy and United Nations Millennium Development Goals (MDGs)

On 29 July 2005 the Commission decided to consult the European Economic and Social Committee (EESC) about reshaping its development policy. In its report, the EESC points out: "Developments on the international stage, new standpoints and consensuses on development policy in the international community and changes within the Union itself suggest that this revision is needed. Likewise, the growing problems of under-development, particularly in Africa, and the increasing differences

---

11 *ACP/EU Courier*, pp. 6–10.

between countries brought about by globalisation underscore the need for a revision of the Community's development policy".[12] The findings of the EESC were not acted upon, and were apparently superseded by a "Joint statement by the Council and Representatives of the Governments of the Member States meeting within the Council, the European Parliament and the Commission", under the heading "The European Consensus on Development". The primary and overarching objective of EU development cooperation was stated as being "the eradication of poverty in the context of sustainable development, including the pursuit of the Millennium Development Goals (MDGs)". In particular, the EU stated its commitment to assist the achievement of the UN MDG of 2000, which were reaffirmed by UN summits in Monterrey (2002) and Johannesburg (2002). The eight MDGs are to:

- Eradicate extreme poverty and hunger
- Achieve universal primary education
- Promote gender equality and empower women
- Reduce the mortality rate of children
- Improve maternal health
- Combat HIV/AIDS, malaria and other diseases
- Ensure environmental sustainability
- Develop global partnership for development.

Apart from joining hands with the UN to achieve the MDGs and restating priorities, the document, produced in typical opaque, generalising, bureaucratic "Eurospeak" contains no fresh ideas or insights beyond what has already been stated and confirmed by NEPAD, the Cotonou Agreement, various G8 resolutions and statements, and United Kingdom prime minister Tony Blair's Africa Commission. Considering that the Council and its member states already decided in the early 1990s to make the fight against poverty one of the main priorities of their development cooperation policies, not much progress, if any, have been made beyond the restatement of problems, re-prioritising, and the formulation of new resolutions. Particularly disappointing about the latest Consensus Document is the little attention (one paragraph) given to lessons of the past, track records of existing programmes and monitoring future implementation. Once again, on the input side of the development equation, particularly

---

12 Opinion of the European Economic and Social Committee on the "Proposal for a Joint Declaration by the Council, the European Parliament and the Commission on the European Union Development Policy – The European Consensus", *Official Journal of the European Union*, 29 September 2005, p. 24.

BOX 5   THE DEVELOPMENT CHALLENGE[13]

"Never before have poverty eradication and sustainable development been more important. The context within which poverty eradication is pursued is an increasingly globalised and interdependent world; this situation has created new opportunities but also new challenges. Combating global poverty is not only a moral obligation; it will also help to build a more stable, peaceful, prosperous and equitable world, reflecting the interdependency of its richer and poorer countries. In such a world, we would not allow 1,200 children to die of poverty every hour, or stand by while 1 billion people are struggling to survive on less than one dollar a day and HIV/AIDS, TB and malaria claim the lives of more than 6 million people every year. Development policy is at the heart of the EU's relations with all developing countries."

impressive data about the volume and relative financial contribution of EU ODA receive high prominence, while nothing noteworthy is said about the output effect or the empirical impact of development policies and aid. Furthermore, no effort is made to address the phenomenon of "aid fatigue", the historical impact of aid on the development of the receiving state, or the debilitating effect of the CAP on the agricultural development of the countries of the South. The EU doubtlessly considers giving development aid as "the right and moral thing to do", but as the apparently faltering UN MDG initiative, the failed promises of the G8 countries and the miniscule financial contributions from donor countries indicate, the unhappy fact is that ODA is still largely a moralistic alibi for the pursuit of self-interest.

Conclusion

EU development aid is a massive undertaking: huge amounts of money are involved, covering an immense geographical area and affecting many millions of people. Apart from the quantitative side, considerable prestige is involved for the donor. Aid to developing countries has become an important tool of foreign policy and national status. From a humanitarian point of view,

---

13   "The European Consensus on Development", Joint statement by the Council and the representatives of the governments of the member states meeting within the Council, the European Parliament and the Commission, 14820/05 (Brussels, February 2006), Annex 1.

what the EU is doing in terms of development aid is indeed laudable. Unfortunately, however, aid is like "shovelling smoke"[14] as it is difficult to correlate inputs with outputs or achievements. What is generally propagated is the quantity of inputs and the money spent, but we seldom hear what happens on the output side of the equation. No calculus seems to exist for this measurement. The general impression is one of inadequacy, of its being too little too late. In spite of the high saliency of Third World poverty and the attention paid to it by the G8, the EU and individual countries, the problem of underdevelopment and all its attendant miseries refuse to subside. In fact, it seems to be getting worse. Yet there seems to be no answer as to how to deal more effectively with the situation and there are apparently no endeavours to find a new way. It leaves the inevitable impression that the prestige and bureaucratic vested interests that have become almost synonymous with development aid are more important than the actual outcome of the effort.

---

14 J. K. Black, *Development in theory and practice: Paradigms and paradoxes* (Boulder, Westview Press, 1999), p. 64.

Chapter 5
The European Union's policy towards democratic South Africa

Introduction

For both the EU and South Africa the mutual relationship that emerged after the demise of apartheid embodied important strategic and symbolic considerations. For South Africa, emerging as it was from a period of prolonged isolation, it was important to establish itself as a "normal" state in world affairs. It had to develop special and beneficial links with the most powerful economic bloc in the world. For the EU, who gave substantial support to the victims of apartheid before 1994, official relations with Pretoria were regarded as a continuation of a policy of constructive engagement with a country that faced the huge challenge of overcoming the aberrations of the past and building a new future. It was important that the miraculous peaceful transformation should not be short-lived and that the positive changes should be permanent and sustainable. EU policies towards South Africa were motivated by this consideration, hence the speedy move to negotiate the TDCA between itself and South Africa and the granting of substantial development aid as part of its policy. At the same time, the EU saw South Africa as a key player in need of support in helping the development of a struggling, unstable and economically backward Southern African region.

The European Union's development policy for South Africa

With the election of a new multiracial democratic government under a new constitutional dispensation a *fait accompli* in South Africa, all previous obstacles to close collaboration with the EU were finally removed. Indeed, in the light of the country's peaceful transformation to democracy and its enthusiastic readmission to the society of nations, the new South African government assumed that the EU and the ACP countries would react with the same cooperative spirit. In October 1994, South Africa formally accepted an EU invitation to work towards a comprehensive and long-term relationship. A Cooperation Agreement to this effect was duly signed by EU Commissioner Leon Brittan and South African Vice-President Thabo Mbeki and subsequently approved by the Council of the EU. The latter agreement also provided a framework for the operation of the EIB in South Africa.

From this point on, the earlier spell of altruism that characterised the EU's approach to South Africa made way for a more competitive and self-centred policy strategy. Although there were various ways in which trade diplomacy between the EU and South Africa could be advanced, discussions centred on two principal options: full or qualified accession by South Africa to the trade provisions of Lomé, or an FTA. The new South African government was keen to enter into a Lomé-based trade agreement with the EU rather than accepting a reciprocal FTA.[1] The Lomé Convention was positioned at the apex of the EU trade accords with countries outside the European Economic Area for three reasons: it covered a wide range of products, the reduction of tariff or non-tariff import barriers tended to be steeper for the items covered under other agreements, and controls were often implemented more sensitively. At the same time, however, the type of FTA proposed came across as equally good as it contained all the best features of various EU agreements.[2] The South African government took the initiative in November 1994 when Vice-President Thabo Mbeki requested the ACP/EU Council of Ministers to open negotiations for South Africa to be included in the Lomé Convention. "In joining Lomé, South Africa only wanted to have access to the General Trade Provisions, and not the special trade protocols [for beef, veal and sugar] or the stabilization mechanism".[3]

---

1 R. Davies, "Forging a new relationship with the EU" in T. Bertelsman-Scott, G. Mills & E. Sidiropoulos (eds), *The EU-SA Agreement: South Africa, Southern Africa and the European Union* (Johannesburg, South African Institute for International Affairs, January 2000), p. 6.
2 See C. Stevens & J. Kennan, with S. Fischer, G. Roberts & R. Rudy, "Trade between South Africa and Europe: Future prospects and policy choices", working paper (Brighton, University of Sussex Institute of Developing Studies, November 1995), p. 25. The country's negotiators, being aware of the problems in "full Lomé membership", actually never explicitly used the term when presenting their case to the ACP/EU Council of Ministers.
3 M. C. Lee, "The European Union-South Africa Free Trade Agreement: In whose interest?", *Journal of Contemporary African Studies*, 20:1 (2002), p. 89.

South Africa's case for joining Lomé also arose from the fact that all its neighbours were members of Lomé and its own membership would facilitate and promote the harmonisation of inter-regional trade and integration in Southern Africa. South Africa sought access only for a transitional period between 1995 and 2000. Its wish to join Lomé was supported by the External Trade Committee of the European Parliament as well as by several ACP countries. But the European Commission (empowered to negotiate trade agreements with third countries on behalf of the EU) rejected full membership and suggested a twin-track approach, specially tailored to South Africa's unique circumstances.

The Commission's proposed twin-track approach entailed firstly, to elaborate a Protocol to the Lomé Convention covering the conditions of accession to the Convention, and secondly, to negotiate a bilateral TDCA between the EU and South Africa, which could lead to the formation of a Free Trade Area. The Protocol was approved by the European Council and the ACP/EU Council in June 1995 and April 1997 respectively, and was duly ratified by the ACP countries and all the EU member states. Formal negotiations between the EU and South Africa were started on 30 June 1995. On 1 June 1998, South Africa was admitted as the 77th ACP Lomé member. Its membership was qualified though. It entailed "all benefits" under Lomé, but excluded non-reciprocal trade preferences and access to the EDF's financial resources. Apparently to soften the blow caused by withholding full trade benefits under Lomé, South African companies were allowed to tender for projects in ACP countries financed under the eighth EDF (valued at a total of ECU 7.5 billion) as of 1 July 1998. Qualified membership also involved South Africa's full participation in the institutions of the Lomé Convention. These include the ACP/EU Council of Ministers, the ACP/EU Committee of Ambassadors, and the ACP/EU Joint Assembly.

From the ACP/EU perspective, there were various reasons why full Lomé trade benefits were withheld from South Africa:
- It was argued that South Africa exceeded the parameters of a "developing country" that made ACP countries eligible for EU membership. Brussels regarded it as a "developed country" and not a "typical" ACP country. While South Africa did indeed share many characteristics with the ACP countries, there were also important qualitative and quantitative differences. It was argued that South Africa was a special case needing a special approach in line with the country's economic position and international trade profile. Lomé was essentially an EU aid programme and an inflexible system of asymmetrical privilege with little man-

oeuvrability for its parties. Compared to the rank and file Lomé member South Africa was a different type of role player. For this reason an FTA with the EU, which included elements of development and cooperation, was regarded as the more propitious route to follow. Lomé was designed to assist the development of some of the world's poorest countries, which South Africa was not, seeing as it had a largely "developed" economy existing alongside a "developing" one. In terms of size and competitiveness its economy outweighed those of the ACP Lomé members by a wide margin. For instance, its total exports to the EU were equivalent to more than a third of the total export of all 70 ACP states combined. At US$120 billion (at the time of negotiations) its GDP was roughly three times the size of the largest economy within the ACP configuration; it also had a GDP greater than four EU countries: Finland (US$104 billion), Greece (US$86 billion), Portugal (US$68 billion), and Ireland (US$53 billion). In the words of Steffen Smidt, Director General for Development in the EU: "South Africa's original request to become a beneficiary to the Lomé Convention's trade arrangements was turned down *inter alia* on the grounds that it could have dwarfed the ACP states in the EU markets. The wider interests of the ACP states have always been a priority for the Union".[4]

- The Lomé dispensation was in any case coming to an end. Lomé IV was due to expire in February 2000 to make way for a new ACP/EU agreement.
- South Africa's agriculture and textile exports could have damaged sensitive EU sectors, and the arrangement would not have been compatible with WTO rules. The controversy regarding WTO compatibility of Lomé would have been aggravated by a decision to grant South Africa non-reciprocal trade preferences. Such an arrangement would stand open to challenge from other WTO members as well as non-ACP developing countries.
- The EU wanted the intended reciprocal FTA with South Africa to serve as a model for its post-Lomé developmental strategy. According to Perry, South Africa's classification as a developed country was a mere technicality, since its *per capita* GNP was lower than several ACP countries. He maintains that the real reason for rejecting the South

---

4 S. Smidt, "The EU's support for regional cooperation and economic integration in Southern Africa", paper presented at the AWEPA Conference on Reconstruction and Democratisation in Southern Africa, Cape Town, 9 September 1996.

African request to the General Trade Provisions of Lomé was fear of competitive South African products. Therefore, it seems that the EU rejected the best option for enhancing economic growth and development in South Africa and the Southern African Development Community (SADC) region.[5]
- Allowing South Africa full access to the Lomé trade regime would have threatened the interests of some sectors of the EU industry, particularly in the agricultural field.
- South Africa's full membership of Lomé might have slowed the pace of dismantling protectionism in the South African economy and pose a serious disincentive to FDI.

At the time of negotiations it had already been clear that Lomé failed to live up to the initial ideals, goals and expectations of its founders. By the time of Lomé IV, it was also obvious that ACP countries were unable to improve their position in global trade. Their food situation deteriorated, standards of good governance and the protection of human rights remained poor and ACP indebtedness was still excessively high. In addition to this, the ACP share of EU trade actually declined over a number of years, falling between 4% and 5% by the early 1990s. Although South African decision makers saw full Lomé membership, particularly access to its General Trade Provisions, as the preferable option, the EU suggested an alternative course: "What we propose is not just an old-fashioned Free Trade Zone. It is nothing less than a Development Free Trade Area, designed to support the South African government in the successful implementation of its economic policies."[6]

However, the devil was in the detail. "The mandate given by the EU Council in March 1996 required its negotiators to seek the exclusion of a long list of products making up some 46 percent of South Africa's current agricultural products to the EU … South Africa might be required to remove duties on around 36% of its current EU imports to secure a mere seven percent in additional duty free access to the market".[7] After much agonising and hand wringing about the best option by the South African side, they finally settled for the TDCA. In the end, this worked out as a sensible and good compromise – probably the best South Africa could have hoped for under the circumstances.

---

5   B. Perry, "Rhetoric and reality? EU policy towards SA 1977–2000", European Development Studies Association (DSA), policy discussion paper no 19, 2000, quoted in Lee, p. 86.
6   Quoted in Lee, p. 86.
7   Davies, "Forging a new relationship with the EU", pp. 7–8.

Negotiating a Trade, Development and Cooperation Agreement between South Africa and the European Union

By the time South Africa and the EU decided to initiate negotiations for the TDCA, the benevolence that marked the latter's aid programme for the victims of apartheid had made way for a more accountable, better managed and better targeted mode of interaction. The lavish allocation of aid money, ostensibly to reward South Africa for getting rid of apartheid, made way for a stricter and more frugal and targeted approach.

This new approach was probably to be expected after the initial international euphoria about the South African "miracle" had dissipated to make way for a more sober assessment of the situation. The EU's lavish aid programme to the victims of apartheid was easy to justify immediately before and during the transition, but the cold reality was that this particular programme was, from a funding point of view, not sustainable for a much longer period. It was not practical either in terms of South Africa's overall development needs at that time or for the future. The EU also realized that it would be problematic to justify to the much poorer and less developed ACP states who were much more dependent on development aid these special benefits to South Africa, a relatively rich country with a relatively developed economy.

Another new reality was the end of the Cold War. At about the same time that apartheid had ended in South Africa, the EU was confronted with a totally new situation in Eastern Europe. The new situation brought to its doorstep new challenges and opportunities that outweighed the importance of all its other foreign policy activities, particularly those in far-flung countries. It became strategically imperative for the EU to bring the former Soviet satellite states in Eastern Europe back into the European fold. The EU had to take advantage of the political and economic opportunities offered by the former impenetrable hinterland that now lay within its grasp and establish the architecture for a more secure future Europe. The staggering cost of additional resources the EU needed in order to prepare the way for the admission and sustenance of its ten new East European members in 2004 are bound to have an adverse impact on the urgency and substance of its ODA programmes with ACP states, which have failed for a considerable period to make the best of the advantages offered by EU ODA. Although the EU studiously refrains from articulating possible adverse consequences of enlargement on ACP countries, it is a realistic and logical expectation that future development policies will be affected.

However, in the midst of all these changes, it was also an important priority for the EU to establish a solid relationship with South Africa. South Africa was regarded as being of special importance in the context of the EU's global range of interests. It offered so much more than the run-of-the-mill ACP country, particularly considering its newly elevated international diplomatic and economic status, the symbolism of its miraculous transition in the context of a struggling and undemocratic Third World, its value as a trading partner, and its role in the Southern African region, in Africa in general, and in the rest of the Third World. This new relationship came into being after a long and arduous negotiation process, stretching from June 1995 to March 1999, and going through 25 rounds of formal negotiations and a large number of informal sessions.

A unique three-pronged model was decided upon: Trade, Development and Cooperation. This approach was different from a one-way street scenario that characterised the ACP/EU Lomé regime; it was one that would benefit both entities more substantially, more directly and more immediately.

This was not what South Africa had wanted most as it had set its eyes on access to the General Trade Provisions of the Lomé Accord. Apart from this, it did not serve its ideological interests as well as full membership of Lomé would have done. At the time of establishing relations with the EU, the ANC government was redefining South Africa's role in the world from the perspective of its liberation struggle. In terms of this new foreign policy, ideological interests came first. The ANC government was particularly wary of compromising its ideological interests and new leadership role in Africa. As a newly liberated country and now the strongest and most advanced country in Africa, it took it upon itself to lead an "African Renaissance" and to help Africa overcome exploitation, marginalization and poverty. In terms of the new foreign policy, Europe and the United States (in fact, the West in general) would not feature at the apex of the ANC's foreign policy value hierarchy. That prime position belonged to Africa and the rest of the Third World. The term Eurocentrism became a pejorative notion in the lexicon of the new ANC establishment, denoting something antithetical to Afrocentrism, a remnant of colonialism as well as a reminder of the erstwhile special relationship with fellow Caucasians in Europe when whites ruled South Africa. Although South African leaders and bureaucrats did not proclaim these extreme sentiments from the mountaintops, they were unmistakably "atmospheric determinants" during South Africa's dealings with Europe and the West at large.

TABLE 3 THE NEGOTIATING PROCESS AND TIMETABLE

June 1995	EU adopts its first mandate and negotiations begin on overall agreement (25 rounds)
March 1996	EU adopts its second mandate on trade
April 1997	Lomé protocol approved
October 1997	Detailed trade negotiations begin
March 1999	Conclusion of negotiations
October 1999	Signing of the TDCA
January 2000	Entry into force of the TDCA

These ideological considerations also formed part of the decision-making milieu when the TDCA was negotiated between the EU and South Africa. To a large extent, they accounted for the competitive nature of the new relationship and the protracted and difficult nature of the negotiation process that followed. Of course, the EU must also share some of the blame for the less than amicable negotiations as its self-centred trade policies contributed in no small way to galvanising ill feelings and scepticism on the South African side.

There were also other secondary reasons for the many muddy patches encountered along the long negotiations path. South African negotiators, short of the negotiating experience and lacking the same power and back-up of their EU counterparts, but very conscious of the new symbolism South Africa stood for, were extremely wary of being outwitted, outsmarted and outdone. At times, the negotiation process came close to a collapse, probably because of gamesmanship and blatant arm-twisting between adversaries who needed one another.[8] The situation was summed up as follows by Michael Laidler, the EU ambassador in South Africa at the time of the negotiations: "To read the newspapers – particularly in South Africa – one would be forgiven for believing that there was a complete stand-off between the parties and that the work of three years was wasted. Indeed, it is true that the final round has been suspended, but paradoxically we are very close to an agreement at a technical level with a few difficult outstanding issues at the political level."[9]

---

8   See in this regard W. Smalberger "Lessons learnt by South Africa during the negotiations" in Bertelsman-Scott *et al.* pp. 47–51. Also see D. Keet, "SA in dangerous waters with EU", *Mail and Guardian*, 29 January–4 February 1999, p. 12.

9   M. Laidler, "South Africa and the European Union: The Free Trade Agreement and Lomé – What can South Africa expect?", seminar report, Europe and South Africa: A Productive Partnership into the Next Millennium, Rand Afrikaans University Centre for European Studies, Johannesburg, 1–2 October 1998 (Johannesburg, Konrad Adenauer Stiftung, 1998), p. 50.

What Laidler referred to centred mainly on agricultural issues such as the interrelation between the Wine and Spirits Agreement and the main TDCA and a Fisheries Agreement. Much acrimony also emanated from seemingly trivial issues such as the use of regional brand names like "sherry", "port", "ouzo" and "grappa" by South African manufacturers. In the end, however, all the technical horse-trading and gamesmanship were of little consequence and an overall balance of interest was agreed upon. Laidler summed up the beneficial side of EU/South African cooperation as follows: "The prize is great for both sides: for Europe a privileged economic and political partnership with the powerhouse of the Southern African region, for South Africa, the strategic and economic medium- to long-term advantages of a special relationship with the world's largest economy".[10] Prominent South African negotiators also concurred that the TDCA was a good agreement that put South Africa in a special and privileged position with the EU when compared to many other nations.[11] According to Links, "the agreement embodies a strategic alliance with South Africa's most important international partner; it is a comprehensive agreement covering a wide variety of trade-related and non-trade areas which provides a framework for investment; and ensures that South-Africa has a special and unique relationship with the EU".[12] In the final analysis, therefore, both sides benefited from the TDCA; but South Africa stood to have suffered most if the negotiations were to have failed. The interdependence factor in the EU/South African relationship weighed heavily in the EU's favour, as South Africa was undoubtedly the more vulnerable party. The power imbalance in the field of trade in particular is illustrated by the fact that the EU accounts for about 40% of the world's imports and exports. By contrast, South Africa represents a tiny fraction of European trading activities. At the same time, however, the EU is South Africa's biggest trading partner, with imports worth R5.5 billion and exports worth R4.1 billion.[13]

The TDCA, which came into effect in January 2000, signalled an important milestone in EU/South African relations. This

---

10 Ibid.
11 R. Davies, "The Department of Trade and Industries perspective", seminar report, South African Business and the European Union in the Context of the New Trade and Development Agreement, Rand Afrikaans University Centre for European Studies, Johannesburg, 18 June 1990 (Johannesburg, Konrad Adenauer Stiftung), p. 40; E. Links, "The European Union-South Africa Trade, Development and Cooperation Agreement and Lomé: The implications", seminar report, ibid. p. 25.
12 Links, p. 25
13 V. Chetty, "Positive spinoffs from the EU trade pact", Business Day: Business Law Review, February 2006, p. 5.

BOX 6 HOW THE TRADE, DEVELOPMENT AND COOPERATION AGREEMENT WILL BENEFIT SOUTH AFRICA AND THE EUROPEAN UNION

Benefits to South Africa
- Forges a strategic, long-term relationship with the EU, the world's largest and most dynamic trading partner
- Reinforces trade links with South Africa's most important trading partner and secures long-term advantages, particularly for industrial products, which form the basis of South Africa's future growth
- Reinforces South African/EU economic and technological links
- Regional economic growth and political stability will be enhanced
- Provides for open-ended assistance to development cooperation, allowing for a greater degree of involvement of the South African government in the application of aid, allowing the programme to be more adapted to South African needs and procedures

Benefits to the European Union
- Further strengthens the close relationship with the EU's single most important economic and political partner in Africa
- Further secures the EU's predominant political and investment position in South Africa
- Provides a working example of EU efforts to provide stability in emerging markets
- Will stimulate and guide the ACP/EU post-Lomé negotiating process
- Will help EU exporters who stand to benefit from substantial South African tariff reductions

agreement became the main pillar of EU/South African relations and defined the new relationship between the two parties. It was an agreement based on mutual interests and strict rules of the game. Both parties would benefit, although an element of asymmetry was introduced in South Africa's favour. No soft concessions were made from either side and nothing was taken for granted, while both parties were ready to put in the necessary effort to make the TDCA a success. Bearing in mind its rather difficult birth process the TDCA is, therefore, not a testimony of a special relationship between South Africa and the EU, but rather a solid legal basis for present and future cooperation.

The substance of the Trade, Development and Cooperation Agreement

In terms of the TDCA, EU cooperation with South Africa takes place under the following headings: Trade and Economic Cooperation; Development Cooperation; and Political, Cultural and Scientific Cooperation. Before 1994, as already explained, the EU channelled aid to South Africa through its Programme for the Victims of Apartheid; after the 1994 democratic elections the institution of the abovementioned programmes superseded it. Three separate sectoral agreements were also negotiated: Science and Technology (signed in December 1996), Wine and Spirits (signed in February 2002) and Fisheries (not yet finalised).

The trade and economic chapter

Trade and economic cooperation between South Africa and the EU takes place under the TDCA (signed in October 1999 and ratified on 1 May 2004). The sectoral Wine and Spirits Agreement was finally signed on 23 February 2002; the only important outstanding matter on the trade negotiations agenda remains the Fisheries Agreement.

The guiding principles of the FTA between South Africa and the EU are asymmetry and differentiation, support for regional integration, WTO compatibility, protection of sensitive sectors, and integration of the South African economy into the global economy. In terms of the asymmetric and differentiation model, the TDCA established an asymmetrical free trade area from 1 February 2000 over the subsequent 12 years between South Africa and the EU, liberalising about 90% of all trade between them. In terms of the agreement, 95% of South African exports would be entering the EU market duty free within ten years and 86% of EU exports would be entering the South African market duty free within 12 years (as from 2000). In addition, the EU undertook to implement its tariff reductions faster with most, though still not all, EU liberalising completed by 2002. On the other hand, South Africa's liberalisation will come into effect between 2006 and 2012. Trade between the two sides will be almost entirely liberalised at the end of this 12-year period. Both sides agreed upon liberalisation schedules reflecting the asymmetrical time schedules for industrial products and agricultural products respectively.

An important parameter that influenced the negotiation process was, of course, the EU's CAP. The protectionism represented by this policy blatantly superseded and contradicted the whole spirit and purpose of an FTA and accounted for much acrimony on both sides during the negotiating process. In the end, the South African side had to accept the CAP factor almost as a *fait accompli*. It had to concede to a formula that excluded 38% of South Africa's agricultural products from the FTA, and which allowed only 21% of such products to enter the EU market upon the commencement of the agreement. The fact that the EU was allowed to bring only 34% of its agricultural products duty free into South Africa did not really level the playing field, as heavy subsidising under CAP allowed various EU products to price South African producers out of the market, causing job losses and reduced incomes in various South African agricultural industries. While both the EU and South African sides pursued their interests in a very competitive manner, the belated and almost ridiculous tug of war the former started about the use of regional brand names like "grappa" and "ouzo" epitomized an extreme protectionist mindset, which South Africans regarded as sheer pettiness.

According to a European Commission publication, "the EU and South Africa have committed themselves to designing the free trade agreement in a way which will support the process of regional economic integration currently underway in the Southern African region".[14] The goal of the TDCA to promote regional integration was perhaps easier said than done. Regional integration is a multifaceted and multidisciplinary process. While both the SACU and SADC represent institutionalised efforts to facilitate the integration process in the Southern African region, the level of integration they represent is still very immature. The EU's Multi-annual Indicative Programme (MIP) (2000–2002) allocated a budget totalling €54.908 million for promoting "Regional Cooperation" (note that the word "integration" is not used). With a few exceptions, these programmes deal with functional deficiencies in the SADC context and with humanitarian problems (like HIV/AIDS), actions that have little to do with the promotion of regional integration *per se*.

From the outset, it was not precisely clear how the FTA would affect members of the Southern African Customs Union (SACU) and members of SADC. Although the South Africans paid lip service to regional interests during the negotiation process, SACU and SADC member countries were excluded from the pro-

---

14 European Commission, "Partners in progress – The EU/South Africa Trade, Development and Cooperation Agreement for the 21st century" (Brussels, Directorate Central Development, October 1999), p. 8.

cess. Moreover, South Africa refrained from consulting its SACU partners (Botswana, Lesotho, Namibia and Swaziland), despite the stipulation of the SACU treaty that this should be done.[15] These countries also stood to suffer as a result of a reduced income from the common revenue pool when the FTA took effect (notwithstanding the realisation that this model of financing was in any case inefficient and unsustainable). Even so, the FTA does contain clauses that are meant to protect the interests of SACU members. These refer to preferential access to the EU under the beef and sugar protocols, and a safeguard clause in favour of infant industries. Products that are of specific interest to the BLNS countries have also been excluded.

Looking at the FTA from a broader perspective, however, it firstly did offer South Africa and the Southern African region the long-term opportunity for and prospect of stronger growth and convergence with higher-income economies, greater integration with international markets and facilitating trade and investment through the creation of larger markets. In addition, it increased the international competitiveness of the EU, which would also spill over to regional economies.[16]

Secondly, the greatest immediate loss to SACU member states will result from the impact of the FTA on the common revenue pool from which they receive the bulk of their budget revenue. Furthermore, in the longer run, they will develop into a captive market for South Africa's non-competitive industrial products, and South Africa will then face the serious demographic and social consequences of economic polarization. The SADC countries that are not SACU members will similarly feel the adverse impact of the FTA, particularly because of the new competition of EU duty free products in the burgeoning informal market in Southern Africa. The MIP (2000–2002) allocated €6 million "to assist the BLNS countries to adjust trade and trade related policies and restructuring of revenue collection in the light of the implementation of the TDCA."[17] However, no disbursement has been allocated.

A third element of the TDCA is WTO compatibility. The EU is satisfied that the FTA met this criterion, because it will cover "substantially all trade" between the EU and South Africa, "without the exclusion of any significant sector"[18].

15　Lee, p. 96.
16　C. Jenkins & L. Thomas, "African regionalism and the SADC" in M. Telo (ed.), *European Union and new regionalism: Regional actors and global governance in a post-hegemonic era* (Aldershot, Ashgate, 2001), pp. 68–169.
17　European Commission, "Partners in progress", p. 8.
18　*Ibid*.

Integration of South Africa into the world economy is the fourth aspect of the FTA. The isolation that the apartheid era brought to South Africa left serious scars on its economy, particularly as far as its economic relations with foreign countries were concerned. According to the EC, the FTA will assist South Africa in its integration into the world economy by helping to promote increased growth and competitiveness, liberalising trade and encouraging investments. It may be too early to judge the outcome of this worthy resolution. Although the South African economy is sound and well managed, growth has remained tardy (in the range of 2% to 3.5%) and FDI has not flown into the country in any meaningful way. Therefore, how and when precisely the FTA will turn things around is yet to be seen.

Although all the objectives of the FTA have not been met equally, difficult barriers have been overcome and in a relatively short period economic relations between South Africa and the EU have grown into one of the main pillars of South Africa's foreign relations. Looking at the quantitative aspect of the FTA, the EU occupies the position of South Africa's most important trading partner, accounting for 40% of its imports, 30% of its exports and close on 60% of its FDI by member states. In a relatively short period after the demise of apartheid, South Africa has become the EU's fifteenth most important trading partner. In 2000, the first year of the TDCA, South African exports to Europe grew by 35%, while EU imports into South Africa grew by 20%. This trend continued in subsequent years, albeit by smaller margins. By the end of 2001, South Africa's trade surplus with the EU had grown from R17 billion in 2000 to R30 billion in 2001, in spite of the steep devaluation of the rand in that year.[19]

However, as table 4 shows, the slowdown in world trade in 2002 also negatively affected trade flows between the EU and South Africa. There was a marginal decline in both EU exports to and imports from South Africa, although the trade surplus of €24 billion is still substantially in South Africa's favour.

Another important instrument of the EU's economic relationship is the Framework Agreement of the EIB, which provides a lending facility to South Africa. Since the first of these agreements was signed in September 1995, lending facilities of €300 million (1995–1997 period), €375 million (1998–2002 period) and €825 million were mandated by the EIB Board of Governors. For all three financial protocols entered into since 1995, committed funds amounted to €1287 million in 2004. Of this amount, 45%

---

19 Delegation of the European Commission in South Africa, Annual Report (2001), Pretoria, p. 2.

TABLE 4 EUROPEAN UNION TRADE WITH SOUTH AFRICA AND EXTRA-EUROPEAN UNION TRADE (IN EURO)

		2001 € millions	2002 € millions	% change (2001–2002)	Jan–Oct 2003 € millions	Jan–Oct 2004 € millions	% change (2003–2004)
Exports EU	To SA	12 480	12 424	-0.4%	11 244	13 432	19.5%
	(Extra-EU total)	974 897	989 170	1.5%	849 463	782 008	-7.9%
	SA as a % of extra-EU	1.27%	1.26%		1.3%	1.7%	
Imports EU	From SA	16 018	15 583	-2.7%	12 375	13 145	6.2%
	(Extra-EU total)	982 428	1 019 191	-3.6%	875 990	819 474	-6.5%
SA as a % of extra-EU		1.56%	1.59%		1.4%	1.6%	9%

Source: Eurostat

TABLE 5 SOUTH AFRICA'S TRADE WITH THE WORLD, 2003

REGION	Imports R billion*	Exports R billion*	Total† R billion
SADC	4.19	26.87	31.06
East and Southern Africa (excluding SADC)	0.24	4.52	4.76
West Africa	3.22	5.99	9.21
North Africa	0.48	1.45	1.93
European Union	109.15	81.72	190.87
Rest of Europe (excluding European Union)	0.44	0.4	0.84
Eastern Europe and Central Asia	7.72	7.29	15.01
East Asia and Pacific	63.63	53.23	116.86
South Asia	3.65	3.89	7.54
Middle East	27.50	8.49	35.99
NAFTA	27.68	27.04	54.72
Americas (excluding NAFTA)	8.7	2.92	11.62
Other	1.57	38.42	39.99
TOTAL†	258.17	262.23	520.4

Source: Industrial Development Corporation
* "Imports" are imports into South Africa, and "exports" are exports from South Africa.
† Figures should add up vertically and horizontally, but may not owing to rounding.

TABLE 6 FOREIGN LIABILITIES (FOREIGN INVESTMENT IN SOUTH AFRICA) AT 31 DECEMBER 2002

Country/ Region	Direct investment R billion	Non-direct investment* R billion	Total R billion†	Proportion of world total	Direct investment as proportion of area total
United Kingdom	158.17	107.41	265.57	36.1%	59.6%
Germany	22.05	22.46	44.5	6%	49.6%
France	3.64	14.12	17.77	2.4%	20.5%
Rest of Europe	27.35	85.86	113.22	15.4%	24.2%
United States	23.88	166.55	190.43	25.9%	12.5%
Rest of North and South America	1.26	5.74	7	1%	18%
Africa	5.47	23.85	29.32	4.05%	18.7%
Japan	3.44	16.42	19.86	2.7%	17.3%
Rest of Asia and Oceania	10.59	13.7	24.29	3.3%	0%
International organisations	—	24.01	24.01	3.3%	0%
TOTAL	255.84†	480.11†	735.95†	100%†	34.8%

Source: South African Reserve Bank
* Includes portfolio investment, and long- and short-term loans from various sources.
† Figures should add up vertically but may not, owing to rounding.

is invested in municipal infrastructure, 16% in the power and gas sector, 15% to support industry (mainly SMEs) and 11% each in the transport and communications infrastructure and the water sector.[20]

The development and cooperation chapter

Chapter 5 of the TDCA deals with European Union/South African development cooperation and sets out the objectives for EU assistance under the EPRD. Programmes are structured and executed in terms of an EU legal base (currently 1726/2000) and an MIP, agreed upon by the EU and the South African government. The programme is the single largest development pro-

---

20 Delegation of the European Commission in South Africa, Annual Report (2004), Pretoria, p. 13.

TABLE 7 FOREIGN ASSETS (SOUTH AFRICAN INVESTMENT IN OTHER COUNTRIES), 1978–2002

	1978 R billion	1982 R billion	1986 R billion	1990 R billion	1994 R billion	1998 R billion	2002 R billion
Direct investment	3.29	6.82	24.08	38.46	67.7	157.39	202.83
Non-direct investment*	4.75	8.57	14.2	16.46	29.96	175.78	449.7
TOTAL†	8.04	15.39	38.28	54.92	97.66	333.17	652.53
Direct investment as a proportion of total	40.9%	44.3%	62.9%	70%	69.3%	47.2%	31.1%
Increase (direct investment)	—	107.3%	253.1%	59.7%	76%	132.5%	28.9%
Increase (direct investment) 1978–2002	—	—	—	—	—	—	6065%
All foreign liabilities vs. foreign assets	289.3%	259.1%	210.9%	163.1%	189.4%	122.8%	112.8%
Direct foreign liabilities vs. direct foreign assets	300.3%	254.5%	90.9%	61.3%	66%	58.4%	126.1%

Source: South African Reserve Bank
*Includes portfolio investment, and long- and short-term loans from various sources.
†Figures should add up vertically but may not, owing to rounding.

gramme in South Africa and the biggest such programme implemented by the EU throughout the world.[21] The MIP is currently worth about €125 million per annum, and so far three such programmes have been approved: 1995–1999, reference amount ECU 650 million; 2000–2002 reference amount €360 million; 2003–2005 reference amount €386 million. For 2006, an additional indicative amount of €129 million is being envisaged, pending an amendment to the regulation (of the EU parliament and the Council) to allow the programme to run over four years instead of the present three years. The focal sectors for support by EPRD funding (€133 million) in 2004 were:[22]

Social services delivery:
- Water Sector Support Programme: €50 million
- HIV/AIDS and Education: €20 million
- Health HIV/AIDS: €25 million

---

21 Delegation of the European Commission in South Africa, Annual Report (1998), Pretoria, p. 10.
22 Delegation of the European Commission in South Africa, Annual Report (2002), Pretoria, p. 10.

TABLE 8 FOREIGN ASSETS (SOUTH AFRICAN INVESTMENT IN OTHER COUNTRIES) AT 31 DECEMBER 2002

Country/Region	Direct investment R billion	Non-direct investment* R billion	Total R billion†	Percentage of world total	Direct investment as percentage of area total
United Kingdom	45.46	178.53	223.53	34.3%	52.4%
Rest of Europe	106.89	96.95	203.84	31.2%	52.4%
United States	22.86	101.69	124.56	19.1%	18.4%
Rest of North and South America	1.91	8.21	10.12	1.16%	18.9%
Africa	14.23	15.78	30.01	4.6%	47.4%
Asia (including Japan)	4.44	6.91	11.35	1.7%	39.1%
Oceania	7	1.24	8.34	1.3%	85%
International organisations	0.03	40.39	40.42	6.2%	0.1%
TOTAL	202.70†	449.70†	652.53†	100.0%	31.1%

Source: South African Reserve Bank
* Includes portfolio investment, and long- and short-term loans from various sources.
† Figures should add up vertically but may not, owing to rounding.

Economic growth:
- Local Economic Development in Eastern Cape: €14 million
- TABEISA 11: €4.9 million

Deepening democracy:
- Transformation of the Justice System: €11 million

Regional integration:
- NEPAD Capacity Building: €2 million

Other interventions:
- Conference, Workshop, and Cultural Initiative Fund: €4.9 million
  – Private sector development: 20%
  – Other (EPRD support facility): 5.2%

The overall objective of South African/EU interaction is typified in the following terms: "to strengthen political cooperation, and to support the SA policies and strategies to reduce inequality, poverty and vulnerability; in the latter context a further aim is to

TABLE 9 EUROPEAN UNION PROGRAMMES IN SOUTH AFRICA, 1995–2001

	Allocated (euro)	Disbursed end 2000 (euro)
Education and Training	154 556 000	94 170 502
Health and Population	116 510 444	56 212 748
Water and Sanitation	111 643 499	83 887 696
Urban Development	182 100 000	70 173 788
Private Sector	95 072 000	20 247 039
EPRD Support Programmes	26 405 796	101 147 606
Good Governance	148 993 900	70 738 207
Regional Cooperation	16 580 100	2 208 874
TOTAL	843 802 340	400 145 182

Source: EC MIP 2003–2005, Annex 1

support SA efforts to mitigate the HIV/AIDS pandemic and its impact on society".[23] Thus, the EU will focus on the following four objectives:
- Equitable access to and sustainable provision of social services
- Equitable and sustainable economic growth
- Deepening democracy
- Regional integration and cooperation.

Cooperation with the South African government is central to the EU's implementation strategy of these objectives. Therefore, the EU commits itself to the following areas of cooperation:[24]
- Supporting the government's implementation of policies and strategies aimed at increasing access to and use of social services for poor people to improve their quality of lives
- Contributing to the acceleration of economic growth, equity and employment
- Enhancing institutional capacity of key stakeholders
- Strengthening the social capital and democratic values with a specific focus on the local level

---

23 European Commission, "South Africa-European Community Country Strategy Paper and Multi-annual Indicative Programme for the period 2003–2005" (Pretoria, Directorate-general for Development, 2003), p. 15.
24 *Ibid.* pp. 15–20.

- Promoting the active participation of South Africa in the regional integration process in the SADC region, and promoting peace, democracy and good governance on the African Continent.

On paper, these programmes look substantial and impressive, but also utterly complicated, if not Byzantine. Moreover, as is the case with all ODA programmes, the correlation between inputs and outputs is vague and uncertain. Aspirations are heavily emphasised while actual achievements are unclear. Attention is being given by the EU and the South African government to the monitoring and evaluation of policy implementation; even so, the overall impact in South Africa is still too vague and difficult to assess because of the absence of reliable outcome indicators.[25] A root cause of the lack of spectacular and visible results is probably the policy of the over-bureaucratisation of development aid and the absence of development science or theory on the planning and implementation sides. The bulk of the EPRD allocation (75%) is channelled through government agencies rather than through more professional, motivated and energetic non-state actors.[26] Other shortcomings seem to lie in the complex and fragmented approach to development, the lack of a scientific approach and an integrated strategy, inadequate staffing, sluggish delivery and poor targeting.[27] The goals of development are not necessarily in harmony with one another and logical sequences of development and reinforcing strategies and tactics should be identified as part of the development strategy. The EPRD seems to work on the assumption that "all the good things will go together", which is mostly not the case.[28]

Political, scientific and cultural cooperation chapter

Political dialogue

The inclusion of the "political dialogue" item in the TDCA (art. 4) may point to the fact that the EU looks beyond the South African "miracle" of 1994, that it is particularly interested and probably

---

25 European Commission, "Evaluation of the European Commission's Country Strategy for South Africa" (Brussels, Directorate-general for Development, 2002), pp. 10–17.
26 See Art. 79–80 of the TDCA.
27 See Jones, p. 426.
28 See S. P. Huntington, "The goals of development" in M. Weiner & S. P. Huntington (eds), *Understanding political development* (Boston, Little Brown, 1987), pp. 3–32.

also concerned about the sustainability and permanence of the South African transformation, and that it wants to secure a role for itself in helping to keep things on track.

The South African transformation came at a time when it was clear that the EU's policies towards the developing world were not meeting the objectives set out. Lomé had been terminated and the Cotonou Agreement was rolled out. South Africa's peaceful political transformation from apartheid to democracy undoubtedly sent out a powerful message to Third World countries: with the necessary leadership and political will, peaceful transformation to a better political order in seemingly hopeless situations was indeed possible. The failure of Lomé to live up to expectations, developments in South Africa, and new post-Cold War global realities called for a paradigm shift in the ACP/EU relationship; hence the change from Lomé to Cotonou.

The EU saw South Africa as a future pole for stability and development in the Southern African region. It wanted its smooth and peaceful transformation to serve as an example for other developing countries still struggling to come to grips with the demands of development, modernity and democracy. In the words of the European Commission, it was looking for a "new thrust in line with a changing world", particularly with regards to globalisation, the information revolution and especially the emergence of a "New Africa".[29] South Africa complied very adequately with the spirit and letter of that idiom, probably more so than any other developing nation. It could serve not only as a testing ground for EU policies, but also as an example to those developing nations still caught up in the anachronistic post-colonial paradigm, which, in the developing nations' eyes, obviated the need for self-correction and new thinking. The EU advocates a break with this paradigm and its stereotypes: "Post-colonial days are over and it is time to stop thinking of donors and recipients, but rather of "common interests to defend"".[30] After the disappointing results of the four Lomé Conventions, the EU was also eagerly looking for a new demonstrable success recipe and South Africa was cast as the perfect role model. When the winds of change started to sweep across the South African political landscape in the late 1980s, the EU wasted no time in becoming

---

29 European Commission, "Southern Africa and the European Union", Series DE 78 (Brussels, Directorate-general for Development, 1994), p. 48.
30 European Commission, "Communication from the Commission to the European Council and the European Parliament on guidelines for the negotiation of new cooperation agreements with the African, Caribbean and Pacific (ACP) Countries" (Brussels, Directorate-general for Development, December 1997), pp. 7–9.

TABLE 10 TOTAL OFFICIAL DEVELOPMENT ASSISTANCE TO SOUTH AFRICA, CUMULATED 1994–1999 (MILLION RAND)

1. EC and EIB	7216	40.81
2. US (USAID)	2498	14.13
3. Sweden	1102	6.23
4. UK	1015	5.74
5. Denmark	919	5.20
6. Germany	831	4.70
7. France	821	4.64
8. Japan	789	4.46
9. The Netherlands	541	3.06
10. Norway	413	2.34
11. United Nations	272	1.54
12. Switzerland	260	1.47
13. Canada	214	1.21
14. China	137	0.77
15. Australia	114	0.64
16. Belgium	113	0.64
17. Italy	105	0.59
18. Finland	103	0.58
19. Ireland	94	0.53
20. International Research Centres	77	0.44
21. Austria	24	0.14
22. New Zealand	15	0.08
23. World Bank	11	0.06
TOTAL	**17 684**	**100**

Source: EC MIP 2003–2005, Annex 2b

involved, starting with substantial assistance to the victims of apartheid. After the transformation became a *fait accompli*, the EU set the ball rolling for the implementation in 2000 of the TDCA under the rules of the World Trade Organisation, which was, in the words of the EC delegation in South Africa, "the furthest of its kind to be signed by the European Union with a third party".[31]

---

31 Delegation of the European Commission in South Africa, Annual Report (2001), Pretoria, p. 4.

South Africa, being an exemplary model of peaceful and democratic transformation, was absolved from the political "conditionalities" that Cotonou imposed on ACP member states. Instead, an element referred to as "political dialogue" was introduced as part of the TDCA of 2000. This insertion provided for "regular political dialogue covering all sides of mutual interest". The agenda for dialogue included:
- Support for democracy and the rule of law
- Respect for human rights and the promotion of social justice
- The creation of acceptable conditions to eliminate poverty and all forms of racial, gender, political, religious and cultural discrimination.[32]

True to its old habits and nature, the EU follows a rather opaque and open-ended methodology with regards to its political dialogue with South Africa. It is a liaison and consultation process that involves the Community's diplomatic delegation in South Africa, the EU presidency and the Community, the South African government, the SADC, and diplomatic representatives in South Africa of EU member states. Its overall objective is to monitor and promote the progress towards stable democracy in South Africa, as well as issues in which South Africa plays a role regionally and globally. Matters that would appear on the agenda are NEPAD, the African Union, and the peace processes in Burundi and the Democratic Republic of the Congo. "The Delegation has accordingly refined its reporting process to the EC headquarters, seeking not only to communicate the South African government's views on issues related to policy environment, but also to widen the information base, while objectively assessing the South African political environment".[33]

For a considerable period, formal political dialogue with South Africa remained in abeyance, ostensibly because of a legal technicality: the ratification process of the TDCA by EU members was not yet complete with Luxembourg (the smallest country in the EU line-up) still not endorsing it. Early in 2004 the process was finally completed. However, according to the EC delegation in South Africa, "political dialogue" in this period occurred "on the margins" at regular meetings of the EU/South African Co-operation Council and with the full consent of South Africa. Matters like the crisis in Zimbabwe, government policy on HIV/AIDS, and peacekeeping in Africa were raised and discussed at these meetings. The impact of these discussions, or to what ex-

---
32 European Commission, "Partners in progress", p. 18.
33 Delegation of the European Commission in South Africa, Annual Report (2002), Pretoria, p. 26.

tent the EU has been and is using its influence to affect outcomes, is not clear. The fact that the government's formerly disastrous HIV/AIDS policy has lately undergone a change for the better must please the EU. But if credit for the change is to be apportioned, it must go to a variety of role players, both local and foreign. The EU's supportive role in the peace-keeping efforts in the Great Lakes Area (where it supplied funding to sustain the South African protective force) was probably more significant: the EU's acting with South Africa and other regional interests increased the chances of success; it was morally the correct thing to do; and the countries and parties involved in the conflict were particularly susceptible to European influence because of historical, cultural and economic ties. However, if Zimbabwe has in fact featured at all in this political dialogue, such discussions have been highly unsuccessful, as the situation there has only become worse with the passing of time. South Africa has been persisting with "soft diplomacy" while the situation in Zimbabwe has got progressively worse, affecting also the rest of the Southern African region. On reflection, it would therefore seem that in problematic cases like Zimbabwe, where the EU is confronted with critical decisions in applying its own norms concerning human rights, good governance, democracy and the rule of law,[34] it has fallen far short, demonstrating its true impotence by allowing the situation to get out of hand.

Prudent conservatives would of course argue that dialogue is just that, and it would be diplomatically inappropriate and indeed risky for the EU to become prescriptive as far as South Africa's domestic or foreign policies are concerned. Given the EU's status as a powerful world economic role player and its relatively substantial investment in supporting and stabilizing the situation in Southern Africa, the question is, however, whether its present role to stop the damage in Zimbabwe is adequate. The limited soft sanctions it did impose against the Mugabe regime have brought little pressure and have been shrugged off as being of slight consequence. Unfortunately, the EU has done little or has been unable to garner multilateral or bilateral diplomatic support for a more assertive regional action plan and strategy to better conditions in Zimbabwe. In the end, the Zimbabwean catastrophe has cost South Africa and the region very dearly financially, politically and morally, in effect nullifying much of the good work and substantial material contributions by the EU to improve things after the regime change in South Africa.

With the remaining legal obstacles now out of the way, the

---

34 See in particular Art. 9 of the "Cotonou Agreement".

EU presidency will dictate the agenda for political dialogue with South Africa. But it seems unlikely that it will give greater thrust to EU actions in troubled areas. Not much should be expected as EU presidents and prime ministers tend to follow their own parochial political instincts and preferences. This was for instance demonstrated by the EU presidency when Italian Prime Minister Sylvio Berlusconi refrained from discussing with Russian President Vladimir Putin, during his official visit to Italy in 2003, Russia's appalling human rights record in Chechnya and its suppression of press freedom.

Scientific, technological and cultural cooperation

South Africa and the European Commission signed an agreement on scientific and technological cooperation in June 1998. The agreement offers South African entities access in all the non-nuclear specific programmes and led to the formation of the Joint South African-European Union Science and Technology Cooperation Committee (JSTCC). The key areas of cooperation are:
- Genomics and biotechnology for health
- Information society and technology
- Nanotechnologies and nanosciences
- Aeronautics and space
- Food safety
- Sustainable development
- Economic and social sciences.

Cultural cooperation does not feature as a priority. The Conference, Workshop and Cultural Initiative Fund (CWCI) disburses €4.8 million and is the only programme in the cultural field. Its basic objective is described to be concerned with improving understanding of the EPRD programme, thus strengthening the European Union/South African partnership through public debate around key issues connected with the MIP.[35] This focus also emphasises the fact that Europe no longer regards it as necessary or important to reach out to elements of Western culture in South Africa, and that common ground is sought more specifically with previous disadvantaged black people in the country. But even with regards to reaching out to the previously disadvantaged, EU efforts are inadequate and generally of little consequence as far as the bigger picture is concerned. A qualitative intellectual interaction between Europe and South Africa hardly

---

35 Delegation of the European Commission in South Africa, Annual Report (2002), Pretoria, p. 46.

exists. This is a rather poignant situation: while the EU strongly emphasises "capacity building" in its programmes, it has no assistance programme to bring promising South African scientists, the "leaders of tomorrow", more regularly and systematically in contact with their European counterparts with a view to develop a stronger scientific/technological knowledge base in South Africa. Systematic European Study programmes exist only at one university in South Africa, while Jean Monnet or related EU sponsored programmes have not been introduced at any of the local or regional universities. At another but related level, the awareness among the South African public and the saliency attached to European matters by the local media remain very low.[36] It is, therefore, rather strange that the EU spends so much on other programmes, while these essential qualitative aspects that could enhance the relationship are practically ignored.

Conclusion

EU involvement in South Africa went through various phases. The first was one of distance and non-involvement. The second phase was characterised by the EU's belatedly joining the UN led international campaign against apartheid in the 1970s and the introduction of a rather ineffective and unconvincing sanctions regime against South Africa. The third phase was introduced in the mid-1980s to support the victims of apartheid by way of substantial financial allocations and supportive programmes. The fourth and present phase, launched after the establishment of democratic rule in South Africa in 1994, brought about the normalisation of relations as well as the intensification of interaction in the fields of trade, development aid, dialogue and partnership by way of the conclusion in 2000 of a comprehensive TDCA. From a diplomatic, economic, developmental and strategic point of view, this is a very important relationship for both the EU and South Africa. The EU is South Africa's biggest trading partner, its biggest donor of foreign aid, and individual members of the EU are the biggest foreign investors in South Africa. The EU, wishing to enhance its role and status in

---

36 Research done by Wadim Schreiner concludes that "between 50% and 60% of television coverage [in SA] is negative... Of special concern is the absence of EU reports in financial media... For any organisation investing such large sums in development projects a measurable output must surely be important... The [media] output for the EU is below measurability and would need urgent improvement". ("Press coverage in South Africa on the European Union", paper presented at SA/EU workshops under the auspices of the Centre for European Studies, Rand Afrikaans University, Johannesburg, 2002).

global matters, puts high value on its relations with South Africa particularly because of the latter's pivotal position in the Southern African region, in Africa in general, in the developing world at large, and in multilateral diplomacy. However, while in diplomatic parlance the relationship is friendly, cooperative and amicable, it is not a very close or special relationship. In the drawn-out negotiations for the all-important TDCA, competition was tough and at times acrimonious, with South Africa having to settle for options less attractive and beneficial than it would have liked. During these negotiations the EU's narrowly defined self-interest dominated. This was in stark contrast to the altruism and goodwill it demonstrated with its magnanimous aid policy towards the victims of apartheid introduced in the mid-1980s and continued with equal commitment after 1994 in support of the new democratic South Africa. On its part, the new ANC led government in South Africa, while actively seeking economic co-operation, aid and trade from the EU, never gave the impression that the latter filled an apex position in its preferred foreign policy hierarchy. This position went to Africa and the rest of the developing world, with whom relations became of great symbolic and ideological importance, although these relations were economically rather insignificant. The new government denounced Eurocentrism (though it does still prevail in South Africa), sending the message that South African/EU relations, while economically important, useful and functional, will never be of a special kind. This policy was most probably meant to signal that the special relations that existed for a long time between Europe and the white South African government helped to perpetuate the status quo and that the new South Africa can never again be comfortable with that epoch in its history.

Chapter 6
Benevolence and self-interest in the European Union's policy towards South Africa

Introduction

The European Union, being an economically powerful multilateral actor with a limited foreign policy mandate plays a rather unique role in world politics, a role that could be interpreted in a number of ways. The rather romantic, idealistic portrayal is that of a benign, apolitical, affluent, stable, peaceful and peace loving role player in the world political arena: it does not threaten states, nor does it compete with them for political gain; it is ideologically neutral and concerns itself primarily with trade, economics, development programmes and humanitarian relief; it is a benefactor of the poor, developing countries, a peacemaker and peacekeeper in world trouble spots, and a promoter of human rights the world over. This depiction serves the foreign policy objectives of the EU. This is the "Venus" image of the EU: a benevolent, gentle giant in world politics who wants to do good in a bad neighbourhood.

To serve EU domestic interests, there is also the "Fortress Europe" characterization, which is almost the polar opposite of the "gentle giant" image. Like a state-actor, the EU seeks to maximize its interests and extend its influence in world affairs; it is an exclusive club of the affluent and relies mostly on the exercise of soft power, particularly economic power, to achieve its foreign policy goals. Its policy is self-centred and exclusive, as epitomised by its miserly executed trade policies and utterly selfish protectionism, particularly through a system of subsidies under its CAP.

In practice, these elements combine to support overall EU foreign policy objectives, rendering its foreign policy a mixture of self-interest and altruism. As a multilateral actor having to operate within the restrictive rules of the Common Foreign and

Security Policy (CFSP) on the one hand and the competitiveness of statecentric power politics on the other, the EU probably regards this two-track strategy as the best available option.

Development assistance serves the self-interests of the EU: it intends to create conditions favourable for trade and economic advancement from which the donor can benefit; it promotes diplomatic influence; it promotes the EU's prestige and image as an international role player in the world; and it serves the growing ambitions of Brussels to conduct its own separate foreign policy. The moral dimension of EU assistance to the developing world also comes into the picture, but in this case it is difficult to distinguish between moral pretentiousness and genuine altruistic concern.

Contrasting the affluence of the EU with the poverty of the Third World, and bearing in mind the relatively small portion of the EU budget that is allocated to ODA and the relatively large portion that goes to subsidising and protecting agriculture in the Community, the conclusion might be reached that its development policy reflects a mixture of things. EU development aid soothes the collective conscience of Europe; it is the morally correct and expedient thing to do. But on the other hand, ODA does reflect the EU's commitment to play a constructive role in a suffering, poverty-stricken and underdeveloped Third World. The EU's ODA policies therefore reflect a complicated mix of morality, expediency, self-interest, altruism, reformism and missionary zeal.

The altruistic/missionary aspect of European Union involvement in South Africa

Trade policy and aid policy in respect to developing nations usually go in tandem. Aid is supposed to promote trade, both directly and indirectly. On the one hand a substantial portion of aid money finds its way back to the donor country. On the other hand, aid is supposed to create a favourable atmosphere between donor and recipient for the promotion of trade, and to promote economic development and growth in the recipient country. In the case of EU aid to South Africa, an additional element of altruism plays a role, mainly because of moral concerns about the plight of the victims of apartheid. Aid was given to help the victims of apartheid without any expectation of reciprocity. In fact, sanctions were applied against the South African government of the time. It could, therefore, be concluded that sentiments among European nations and in the EU prescribed that action be taken because at the time it was thought to be the right thing to do. As already indicated, substantial contributions were made by the EU over a number of years, although it is not clear to what extent these contributions helped to sway the favour of the new government towards the EU.

At large it does not seem that the impact of EU diplomacy on South Africa's general attitude was significant by any manner or means. The negotiations between the EU and South Africa for an FTA were conducted in an utterly competitive and at times even acrimonious spirit and although a good compromise was reached in the end, the two entities never entered into a special relationship. Even so, to the satisfaction of both parties, the FTA boosted reciprocal trade considerably, which will probably continue irrespective of ODA from the EU.

Being constitutionally restricted to a largely non-political role in global affairs leaves the EU little choice but to pursue a soft diplomatic strategy in its foreign policy. Thus, in contrast to the generally self-serving and highly competitive nature that characterise conventional interstate bilateral relations, the rationale of the EU's policy towards South Africa reflects a dualism. On the one hand, its trade policy is fiercely competitive, but on the other hand, its development assistance policy at least outwardly reflects an altruistic-cum-idealistic style and posture. On the non-trade side of the relationship, the EU studiously refrains from articulating its policy objectives towards South Africa in the concrete terms of self-interest, preferring instead to explain its role in the rather ubiquitous and idealistic terms of "what is good for South Africa". Explanations of EU goals in South Africa generally emphasise the normative and reformative aspects of its activities such as sustainability, capacity building, stability, socio-economic development, poverty relief, support for democratisation and promotion of human rights.

The following policy explanations by the European Commission and its agents have become standard since the beginning of their involvement in South Africa:

- "[The] European Union has made a commitment to maintain and even strengthen its support to South Africa's political, economic and social development".[1]
- "The rationale of EU cooperation is based on the assumption that South Africa is a pole of stability in the Southern African region, which deserves to be supported and strengthened".[2]

---

1 European Commission, "Country Strategy Paper for South Africa (2000–2002)" (Brussels, Directorate-general for Development, 1999), p. 3.
2 European Commission, "Evaluation of the European Commission's Country Strategy for South Africa", p. 5.

- "The overall objective of EU aid to South Africa from 1986 to the present has been to assist the country and its people in a peaceful transition to a stable, democratic, non racial and prosperous society".[3]
- "Development co-operation shall contribute to South Africa's harmonious and sustainable economic and social development and to its insertion into the world economy and to consolidate the foundations laid for a democratic society and state governed by the rule of law in which human rights in their political, social and cultural aspects, and fundamental freedoms are respected. Within this context, priority shall be given to supporting operations which help the fight against poverty".[4]
- "[T]he overall objectives we have followed remain good: to strengthen political cooperation, and to support the SA policies and strategies in order to reduce inequality, poverty and vulnerability; the new factor is the AIDS pandemic which requires us to renew our effort to support SA to mitigate its effects and its impact on SA society".[5]

The EU also justifies its role in South Africa in regional terms, ostensibly because of its important stake in the success of the Cotonou Agreement and the pivotal position South Africa occupies in this regard.[6] According to the EC's Country Strategy Paper for South Africa 2000–2002, "the rationale for EU involvement is based on the assumption that South Africa is a pole for the development of peace, democracy and democratic growth for the entire Southern African region. If South Africa is to play this role, it must still overcome major social and economic challenges which have started to be addressed in the last five years."[7]

The current legal base of the EU's development assistance programme, chapter 5 of the TDCA, is furnished by Regulation (EC) No 1726/2000 of the European Parliament and Council (29 June 2000). In this important document the *raison d'être* of EU involvement in South Africa is articulated as follows:

> The Community shall implement financial and technical cooperation with South Africa to support the policies and reforms carried out by the South African authorities in a

---

3 European Commission, "Country Strategy Paper for South Africa (2000–2002)", p. 1.
4 Quoted by L. Fioramonti, "The European Community promoting human rights and democratic consolidation at micro-level: The case of South Africa", paper delivered at IPSA Conference, Durban, June–July 2003, p. 10.
5 Laidler, p. 50.
6 See Smidt.
7 Laidler, p. 4.

context of policy dialogue and partnership. The aim of the Community cooperation programme ... shall be to contribute to South Africa's harmonious and sustainable economic and social development, through programmes and measures designed to reduce poverty and encourage economic growth which benefits the poor, and to its continued integration into the world economy, and to consolidate the foundations laid for a democratic society and a State governed by the rule of law in which human rights and fundamental freedoms are fully respected. This will be achieved through support for international targets and policies for sustainable development based on UN conventions and resolutions, thereby contributing to the target of reducing by at least one half the proportion of people living in extreme poverty by 2015.

European Union self-interest in its relations with South Africa

The above motivations stress the idealism and almost missionary fervour that underpin the EU development policy towards South Africa. Of course, these explanations of ODA policies are not unique to the EU, as donor countries generally do the same when seeking to justify their foreign aid policies to audiences at home and abroad. According to Black, "development is a user-friendly term, having virtually as many potential meanings as potential users. If there is a commonality among its many uses, it might be in denoting enhancement, that is, increasing value or desirability; but that leads us once again to subjectivity".[8]

Varieties of altruistic considerations play a role in most cases, but so do moral pretentiousness and egocentric self-interest. Among these, self-interest is usually the dominant objective: all donors of ODA regard it as an instrument of foreign policy and a tool of national interest. The fact that the EU is a multilateral body does not alter the situation; self-interest also plays an important role, albeit in a subtler and less conspicuous way as in the case of bilateral aid. Aid and trade, self-interest and idealistic altruism, therefore, reinforce one another as instruments of EU foreign policy. While its ODA policies are usually clothed in the patronizing and benevolent style of altruistic sincerity, the parallel strategy on the trade side of relations is utterly competitive and self-explanatory.

---

8 Black, p. 15.

The fact that the EU Commission in Brussels is not accountable to a popular constituency gives it much more leeway than is the case with donors of bilateral aid. This may account for the fact that some of its "development" projects in South Africa border on the romantic and portray the extent of EU affluence. But EU development assistance also presents an impressive picture of commitment and professional performance. Concrete evidence indicates that its contribution to South African development is unequalled in comparison to the contributions of other role players. The total ODA to South Africa amounted to R17.684 billion for the period from 1994–1999, the EU contribution of which was R7.216 billion, or 40.81%.[9]

The EU's per capita contribution of development aid in South Africa is the highest of all its programmes in the developing world. Over a period of almost two decades, the EU has demonstrated the sustainability of its commitment not only by remaining involved, but also by constantly endeavouring to add substance and sophistication to its involvement.

Of course, it is still much too early to assess the actual and overall impact of these programmes on South Africa's progress towards stable democracy, accelerated and sustained development, and modernization. In the end the litmus test will lie in what these indicators tell us in concrete terms. However, while this aid policy is in progress, it promotes the image and prestige of the donor, and as such, its self-interest. Success, if it comes, is an additional bonus.

The harder, business-like side of the EU's commercial policy came strongly into the foreground during the extended and difficult bargaining process that marked the birth of the TDCA with South Africa. Acrimony aroused by seemingly trivial issues such as the South African usage of European regional brand names ("grappa", "port", "sherry" and "ouzo") almost scuttled the process, while the EU efforts to muscle in on securing fishing rights in South African waters showed the sharp competitive side of the relationship. According to Davies: "Trade relations with the EU involve hard bargaining, in which professed concerns to promote development and greater equity in trade relations with developing countries are often swamped by what the *Financial Times* called 'commercial haggling by wealthy Europeans'."[10] When it comes to trade and trade policy, the EU switches roles and becomes the relentless competitor. When comparing the

---

9 European Union, Development Cooperation Report 2000, quoted in the addendum to the "South Africa-European Community Country Strategy Paper and Multi-annual Indicative Programme for the period 2003–2005", (Brussels, Directorate-general for Development, 2003), Annex 2b.
10 Davies, "Forging a new relationship with the EU", p. 11.

EU's trade policy and its development policy, it seems to be a case of self-interest juxtaposed against altruism. Obviously, this is all part of a European philosophy and grand strategy. But whether it works as well in practice is another question, as the Lomé experience has validated so clearly.

As demonstrated by the EU's long uncompromising stance (recent declarations indicate policy shifts) on the CAP as well as its self-centred approach with regard to trade disputes and tax regimes in general, self-interest weighs heavily in favour of EU trade and general economic advantages of "Fortress Europe". Its prolific involvement with the promotion of growth and stability in ACP countries also reflects a strong element of self-interest: the advantages of a captive market, unrestricted access to raw materials, lucrative income and employment opportunities for EU nationals from tenders, contracts, service charges, consultation fees, etc., are usually not emphasised in policy statements, but they undoubtedly serve the national interest more than anything else. From the very beginning the EU's involvement in ACP trade and development cleverly combined moral obligation towards the poor ex-colonial countries with self-interest in the sense that it was good for European business, European welfare, European diplomacy and the European world image. The disappointing outcome of the four Lomé Conventions was probably more harmful to the ACP countries than to the EU. Although the Cotonou Agreement introduced changes to the Lomé model, these changes were more cosmetic than fundamental. The EU policy makers and strategists seem to prefer the imperfect status quo to a fresh approach that deviates from the "Washington consensus" and caters better for the real problems and interests of the ACP states. EU strategists are reluctant to revisit, intellectually and theoretically at least, the entire problem of development and modernization in developing countries and switch gears to a more relevant approach in the post-Cold War era. The changes they do make, as reflected in Cotonou, are mostly of a technical and bureaucratic-administrative nature. To underline the importance of their role, they continue to place much emphasis on the staggering sums of money being allocated and spent, and how favourably EU aid packages compare with those of other donors. However, at the same time, the much more important output side of the developmental equation, i.e. outcomes and problem solving, is either neglected or inadequately analysed and explained.[11]

---

11 See M. Bratton & C. Landsberg, "From promise to delivery: Official Development Assistance to South Africa, 1994–8", research report no. 68, ad hoc publication, (University of the Witwatersrand Centre for Policy Studies, Johannesburg, 1999).

Conclusion

The EU, being a multilateral organisation and non-state actor with a limited role in world politics and whose members make their own foreign policies, has a special, rather unique, role in world politics. It is generally regarded by states as a benign role player in the political arena: it does not threaten them and does not compete with them for political gain. For all intents and purposes, the EU is regarded and treated as an ideologically neutral organisation by nation states the world over. Yet, in spite of these perceptions, the EU is not a totally apolitical organisation. Brussels, in its own particular way, seeks greater influence as a non-state actor, and recognition in world affairs. For this reason it engages in development assistance on a very wide scale; is involved in peacekeeping exercises in various parts of the world; participates in humanitarian assistance programmes; encourages and promotes regionalization in other parts of the world; and actively protects and promotes human rights the world over. At the same time, the European Commission, with its being in control of EU trade relations and the EU's being the biggest single trading bloc in the world, is a prominent and incisive role player in global trade and the formulation of global trade policies. This dual aid and trade role is not necessarily compatible: unpopular trade policies, like protectionism and particularly the discriminatory subsidy system of the EU's Common Agricultural Policy, clearly clash with its good intentions of helping the developing countries of the Third World. Especially the negotiations leading to the conclusion of the TDCA with South Africa demonstrated the hard-nosed pursuance of self-interest on the part of the EU when its own economic interests come into play. It is indeed hard to reconcile the liberal benevolence of the EU's post-1985 aid programmes to the victims of apartheid, and after 1994 to the new democratic South Africa, with the unrelenting and narrow-minded pursuance of trade interests. In the end, the conclusion of the TDCA was to South Africa's advantage as well, but on the terms laid down by Brussels.

Considering the parameters and realities of North-South relations and the realities of the EU, particularly its agricultural protectionist policies, the TDCA is a very good agreement for South Africa. It covers much more than merely trade: it forms the basis for forging a comprehensive, long-term strategic relationship between South Africa and the EU. At the same time, it is also a new form of trade arrangement for South Africa – a bilateral FTA with the largest and one of the most developed trading blocs in the world, providing South African industrial products with improved access to the EU market. It provides a basis for attracting new investment by both domestic and foreign investors in industries seeking to use South Africa as a springboard to enter the European market. While it is clear that the TDCA opened a variety of windows apart from the trade side for cooperation in the fields of services, communication, health, and broadly defined "economic cooperation", the ball has very much been placed in the South African court to make the most of these. Although the spirit in which the TDCA was negotiated was at times acrimonious and marked by haggling to promote the vested interests of EU lobbies, it was in the end a significant achievement, a milestone in South Africa's foreign relations and of huge importance to its overall national interests. The TDCA no doubt marked an important symbolic and strategic achievement for the EU too (see later), but in relative terms in the total order of things, it was not nearly as vital to the EU as it was to South Africa.

Therefore, although one would have expected that the agreement inaugurated an era of a new special European Union/ South African relationship, it did not turn out that way. This development is naturally not in South Africa's best interest. In the final analysis the EU is a vital source of national wealth and welfare in a society where poverty, unemployment and deprivation are still rampant.

Chapter 7
The regional context of South African/European Union/African relations

Introduction

Both the EU and South Africa have strong and vested interests in regional integration in Africa. The reason for these interests is that both believe that regional integration in Africa is the best way to achieve peace, security and economic development on the continent. Since South Africa's regime change in 1994, regional cooperation in Africa has become a centrepiece of the new government's foreign policy. It has assumed a leadership role in the New Partnership for Africa's Development (NEPAD) and the African Union (AU) and made special efforts, albeit not very successfully, to resuscitate the role of the SADC and to add greater legitimacy and efficiency to the SACU. On its part the EU introduced a strong new emphasis on regional development and cooperation, particularly with the conclusion of the Cotonou Agreement. In addition, the EU has actively supported African regional initiatives by way of development aid and diplomatic initiatives, focussing on closer cooperation with the continent.

European Union promotion of regional cooperation and integration in Southern Africa

Being a singular successful experiment in regional integration, it is logical to think that the EU model could also help Africa to overcome its mountain of problems. Although some African leaders made this deduction at the formation of the African Union, Brussels has never explicitly articulated this scenario. Even so, the EU has in recent years adopted a strong and positive attitude towards regionalization efforts on the African continent. It regards regional integration as the best road towards development, modernization, peace, and stability in Africa. Such a development would without a doubt also serve the interests of the EU. A stable and prosperous continent would benefit EU trade, give greater meaning and impact to development aid, and underscore the general political and strategic importance of Africa for Europe and the West at large.

The promotion of regional integration is listed as a priority in the new ACP/EU Partnership Agreement, signed in Cotonou in 2000, and the goal and purpose of successive MIPs are to provide "support to integration and cooperation processes at NEPAD, SADC and SACU level, with specific attention to the regional dimension of the focal areas of cooperation with South Africa". For the period from 2003–2005, an indicative amount of €50 million was earmarked for support to "regional integration and cooperative intervention",[1] continuing the contributions of preceding MIPs.

Present EU assistance towards regional integration consists of programmes to increase regional trade, to improve efficiency in the use of transport and communications, to improve water resource management, to improve (with cooperation of the World Health Organisation) access and quality control of essential pharmaceutical products, to participate in conflict prevention and resolution with a programme aimed at consolidating peace and democracy in Southern Africa, and to help SACU members to deal with the implications of the TDCA.

Regional engineering in Africa: The search for a better way

Regionalism is not a new phenomenon in Africa. The SACU is the oldest customs union in the world, and "the list of both past and present multilateral economic agreements [in Africa] is probably longer than of any other continent"; even so "Africa's record of creating and sustaining regional frameworks is generally poor."[2] In view of the EU's undoubted success and its potential as a role model, a better understanding of the way it came about, its structures and functions, and its successes and failures are of great importance to African regional engineering.

African regionalization is still very immature and shallow measured in terms of the general criteria of integration and par-

---

1 *Bratton & Landsberg.*
2 Jenkins & Thomas, p. 153.

BOX 7 PRINCIPLES OF THE AFRICAN UNION (ARTICLE 4 OF THE CONSTITUTIVE ACT)

- Sovereign equality and interdependence among member states of the Union
- Respect for borders existing on achievement of independence
- Participation of the African peoples in the activities of the Union
- Establishment of a common defence policy for the African continent
- Peaceful resolution of conflicts among member states of the Union through such appropriate means as may be decided upon by the Assembly
- Prohibition of the use of force or threat to use force among member states of the Union
- Non-interference by any member state in the internal affairs of another
- The right of the Union to intervene in a member state pursuant to a decision by the Assembly in respect of grave circumstances, namely war crimes, genocide and crimes against humanity
- Peaceful co-existence of member states and their right to live in peace and security
- The right of member states to request intervention from the Union in order to restore peace and security
- Promotion of self-reliance within the framework of the Union
- Promotion of gender equality
- Respect for democratic principles, human rights, the rule of law and good governance
- Promotion of social justice to ensure balanced economic development
- Respect for the sanctity of human life, condemnation and rejection of impunity and political assassination, acts of terrorism and subversive activities
- Condemnation and rejection of unconstitutional changes of governments

ticularly when compared to the achievements of the EU. This is despite the fact that African regionalization receives constant high-level political attention and has indeed become a matter of great saliency since the formation of the OAU. At the same time, as already pointed out, both South Africa and the EU have become important role players in African regionalization, albeit for different reasons.

While African regionalization is in a process of evolution, an important question is whether the EU could indeed serve as a role model for African regionalization. From this perspective, a closer look at and a comparative analysis of the salient dimensions of the EU and regional organisations in Africa, especially the AU, are essential. Convergences and differences between these two regional endeavours and the relevance of the EU to Africa need to be discovered.

The "idea of Africa" and the "idea of Europe"

An important element promoting integration in both Europe and Africa is a pre-existing sense of identity, unity and cohesion, best typified as the "idea of Europe" and the "idea of Africa". However, in spite of a strong "we-feeling" among African states, their willingness to "shift their loyalties, expectations and political activities toward a new centre, whose institutions possess or demand jurisdiction over the pre-existing national states"[3] is largely absent. Of course, not even EU member states conform to all these criteria, although they are generally more inclined than African states are to pool sovereignty on a variety of issues.

The evolving identity of Europe dates back many centuries, perhaps as far as the first Christian Roman emperor, Constantine (312–337), and more specifically to the year 800 when Pope Leo III crowned Charlemagne as Holy Roman Emperor. The idea of a "Federal Europe" or a "United States of Europe" has enjoyed the attention of various prominent European idealistic philosophers since the 18th century. These idealists saw Europe "as one great republic" with a "common moral and intellectual outlook".[4] The recurring theme in the writings of intellectuals like William Penn, Abbé de Saint-Pierre, Jeremy Bentham, Immanuel Kant, Jean-Jacques Rousseau and Victor Hugo was "perpetual peace". However, their outcry has been totally in vein as they were unable to stem the tide and the consequences of inward-looking territorial nationalism that engulfed Europe after the French Revolution.

Apart from the period of peace secured by the balance of power, underpinned by a rather flimsy moral consensus and aristocratic horse trading during the Concert of Europe period (1812 to 1914), Europe was a house divided allowed to go to rack and ruin through intermittent wars and continuous crises. Not

---

3 *Ibid.*
4 H. J. Morgenthau, *Politics among nations: The struggle for power and peace* (New York, Alfred A. Knopf, 1973), p. 221–222 (quoting Edward Gibbon and Arnold Toynbee).

even the horrors of World War 1 were enough to move the political elite establishment or mass politics in Europe to embrace a new paradigm based on greater European unity and supranational cooperation. The catalyst for radical change was World War 2, when the inability of Europe's nation states to resist dictatorship and extremist nationalism were demonstrated so glaringly. These shortcomings were, however, not the only reasons for shifting to a new paradigm. There were also questions about Europe's economic future, which Count Coudenhove-Kalergie, leader of the Pan-European Movement, articulated as follows: "Can Europe preserve its peace and its autonomy in the face of growing non-European world powers, if she remains politically and economically divided, or is she forced to organise herself as a federation of states to save her existence?"[5]

Over the years, the notion of a "united Europe" developed into a remarkably resilient symbol, so that "individuals of Conservative, Liberal and Social leanings have no difficulty in embracing it".[6] Yet Europeans of different nation states showed a steadfast reluctance to transfer loyalty to supranational institutions. Also, while European governments, political parties and interest groups embraced the idea of a "united Europe", it never developed into a single doctrine of consensus. It meant different things to different people and was adapted according to different philosophical dispositions and vested interests. Indeed, political parties in all European countries harbour adherents as well as opponents to the symbol. Certain factions support federalism while others remain ardent supporters of the sovereign supremacy of the nation state system.

Although the "idea of Africa" is of much more recent origin than the "idea of Europe", it has been an equally powerful force in the shaping of Africa's destiny. Pan-Africanism is a major manifestation of the African idea. Whereas the quest to end long-lasting nationalistic conflicts forced Europeans to greater unity, pan-Africanism was, at least in its early stages, nurtured, conceptualised and promoted by Africans of the diaspora in the West Indies and the United States of America. According to Vincent Bakpetu Thompson, pan-Africanism "reflects the endeavour of Africans to establish some bulwark against the inroads which people of European origin made on their lives."[7] When colonialism came to an end in the 1960s, some leaders, particularly Ghana's Kwame Nkrumah, argued that Africa could only sur-

---
5 M. O'Neill, *The politics of European integration* (London, Routledge, 1996), p. 14.
6 E. B. Haas, *The uniting of Europe: Political, social and economic forces* (Palo Atto, Stanford University Press, 1958), p. 20.
7 V. B. Thompson, *Africa and unity: The evolution of pan-Africanism* (London, Longman, 1969), p. 18.

vive as a single united entity. Others like Félix Houphouët-Boigny of Côte d'Ivoire maintained that the newly independent countries must first build strong nation states. The OAU was created as a compromise between these two viewpoints.[8]

Africa has managed to liberate itself from the scourges of slavery, colonialism, imperialism and racism. African unity and African fraternity have become major tenets in not only intra-African relations, but also vis-à-vis the outside world. Like Europeanism, pan-Africanism contains many paradoxes and serves many purposes. But while heterogeneous thinking about the structural and functionalist aspects of integration underpins Europeanism, pan-Africanism is a monolithic idea and ideal as far as African leadership is concerned. This was reflected in the charter of the OAU, founded in 1963. Article 2 stated the purposes of the OAU as follows: "(a) to promote unity and solidarity of the African states; (b) to coordinate and intensify their co-operation and efforts to achieve a better life for the peoples of Africa; (c) to defend their sovereignty, their territorial integrity, and independence; (d) to eradicate all forms of colonialism in Africa; and (e) to promote international cooperation, having due regard to the Charter of the United Nations and the Universal Declaration of Human Rights."

In this formulation, Africa was seen as a community of sovereign independent nations, rather than a community of Africans irrespective of national origin. The Westphalian principles which European nations have been trying to get away from by pooling their sovereignty, took a central place in the African political philosophy as expressed in the OAU. After the end of the Cold War, with the emergence of globalisation, and with colonialism and apartheid out of the way, the OAU became a largely dysfunctional, if not anachronistic organisation. While the mythical force of "African unity" continued to permeate African politics, commitment to unity alone could not prevent the continent from slipping into crises of international political irrelevance, marginalization and economic decay. Perhaps the OAU's greatest failures were that it could not move beyond the post-colonial *status quo*, that it tolerated political and economic decay in deference to sovereign independence and fraternal unity, and that it failed to secure intra-African peace, good governance and democracy. The clearest admission of Africa's existential crisis and the dysfunctionality of the OAU came from South African President Thabo Mbeki's launching of the African Renaissance initiative, soon to be followed by the replacement of the OAU with the AU

---

8   Wikipedia, "Africa Union", C:%20Union%20-20-%20 Wikipedia,%20the %20%free%2Encyclopedia.htm.

and the implementation of NEPAD and the African Peer Review Mechanism (APRM).

Europe's incrementalism versus pan-African grand design

One important difference between the integration processes in Europe and Africa is the dynamic bottom-up, step-by-step, open-ended process of the former, as opposed to the top-down, rigid, almost glacial nature of the latter. European integration is an exercise in pragmatism to achieve peace and progress while African integration, at least until the coming of the AU and NEPAD, was mainly ideologically driven to protect the gains of the struggle against colonialism and apartheid. Currently, African integration efforts as envisaged by the AU Act and NEPAD are based on idealistic grand designs where a multitude of organs and complex structures are tasked to achieve a broad spectrum of objectives, seemingly with the assumption that noble notions automatically ensure success.

The EU, on the other hand, shunned the idea of European integration linked to one political all-inclusive concept. As Robert Schuman put it in the famous declaration of 9 May 1950, "Europe will not be made all at once or according to a single plan. It will be built through concrete achievements which will first create real solidarity."[9]

Another major difference between the African and European approach to integration is the membership policy. Africa follows an inclusive approach, while Europe follows an exclusive membership policy. According to Article IV of the OAU charter, "Each independent sovereign African state shall be entitled to become a member of the organization". The AU Act stipulates in Article 29 that any African state shall become a member if a simple majority of the member states votes in its favour. No qualitative criteria are required at all. Members can be undemocratic; they can be economically weak, badly administered and corrupt; they are not required to show respect for the rule of law or to not discriminate against minorities; they can even be in a state of war against fellow-members or experiencing a revolution.

EU membership rules are infinitely more strict and complex. On the one hand, membership is an act of political discretion, particularly by the European Council and the member states, but on the other hand very strict and cumbersome socio-political criteria and legal requirements have to be met by applicant states.

---

9   Cited in McCormick, p. 12.

For instance, undemocratic regimes are completely unacceptable. This was the case when Spain under the Franco dictatorship and Portugal under the Caetano dictatorship unsuccessfully applied for associate membership in 1962. Membership applications for Spain and Portugal were only taken seriously when the authoritarian regimes were removed and replaced by democratic ones. The so-called "Copenhagen criteria" lay down the specific economic and political pre-conditions for membership:

- Stable democracy and its underpinnings (rule of law, multiparty system, respect for human rights, protection of minorities, pluralism, etc.)
- A functioning of a market economy that will be able to deal with the pressure of competition
- The ability to assume the rights and obligations arising from Community law
- Adherence to the aims of political union
- The EU's capacity to absorb new members without impairing its integrative momentum.[10]

Even if these conditions are met, a political decision (an absolute favourable majority by the European Parliament and ratification by member states) is still required. After that, a Treaty of Accession is put in place and the primary and secondary legislation (*acquis communautaire*) obtain the force of law in the new member state.

The difference in the respective admission criteria of the AU and the EU explains many of the reasons for the success of European integration and the lack of success of African integration, at both continental and sub-regional levels. But then the question arises as to whether integration along the lines of the EU model could really be a serious goal of intra-African politics and economics. Like the OAU, the AU places its main focus on the achievement of greater unity and solidarity between the African countries, and on the defence of sovereignty, territorial integrity and independence of member states. These two goals are clearly irreconcilable when measured against the salient requirements of regional integration.

Statecentrism vs. supranationalism in Africa and Europe

In various degrees, both Europe and Africa still cling to the traditional Westphalian paradigm of national sovereignty. However,

---

10 Weidenfeld & Wessels, p. 94.

Africa's commitment to this paradigm is total, while in Europe the notion of shared sovereignty between the Community and individual states is gaining ground, albeit with great difficulty. Europe's rejection of a single integration plan had much to do with the abiding power of the nation state, elite resistance and the unpreparedness of public opinion to take a bold step by moving from the statecentric confederalism to supranational federalism as a mode of integration. Although it was realized after World War 2 that the nation state in its traditional form could no longer protect its citizens, and that it was in fact one of the causes of the war, the supranationalists failed to muster the necessary political will and public support to dispense with it. In Europe, as in Africa, therefore, irreconcilability between national sovereignty and supranationalism remains a formidable stumbling block in the way of integration.[11]

But in contrast to Africa, Europe has found practical ways to circumvent the stranglehold of xenophobic nationalism. While federalism could despite its many talented articulators not find the favour of governments and elites in Europe, a compromise was found in David Mitrany's functionalist approach. This was not regarded as an immediate threat to the sovereignty of the nation state. Building on the Mitrany theory, Jean Monnet, Robert Schuman, and later Paul Henri Spaak, with the cooperation of Europe's erstwhile main rivals, Germany and France, managed to introduce functionalism by way of the European Coal and Steel Community (ECSC), which came into being after the Treaty of Paris in 1951. As Monnet explains: "The ECSC suggested a way of integrating Europe by stealth, without directly confronting the interests, offending the national sensibilities or compromising the identity of the existing nation state authorities .... Little by little the work of the Community will be felt .... Then the everyday realities will make it possible to form the political union which is the goal of our Community and to establish a United States of Europe .... The unification of Europe, like all peaceful revolutions, takes time."[12]

The ECSC established exactly what Schuman and Monnet had anticipated. Apart from a period of stagnation, also referred to as "eurosclehrosis", remarkable progress was made between the establishment of the ECSC and the 1992 Treaty of the European Union (TEU) concluded in Maastricht. This process "to-

---

11 See *inter alia* A. W. Cafruny & C. Lankovsky (eds), *Europe's ambiguous unity: Conflict and consensus in the post-Maastricht era* (London, Lynne Rienner, 1997), pp. 1–67; B. Burrows, G. Denton & G. Edwards (eds), *Federal solutions to European issues* (London, Macmillan, 1977); Nelsen & Stubb, pp. 189–334.
12 Quoted in O'Neill, pp. 35, 36.

wards ever greater union" goes on as EU membership is extended and constitutional and functional innovation continues. A significant feature of this progress is the absence of a single dominant paradigm of European integration. Instead an ambiguous, syncretic or hybrid paradigm prevails. Features of supranationalism (federalist and functional models) as well as of statecentrism (intergovernmentalism and confederalism) are prevalent as the European integration process responds to a mixture of impulses.[13] According to Devuyst: "Via the Treaties of Paris (1951) and Rome (1957) the Member States established a new policy capable of producing and enforcing binding European Community law through its institutions and decision-making mechanisms." This "Community method" goes well beyond the traditional intergovernmental set-up. It places the European Community formation apart from other intergovernmental organisations like the United Nations and other regional formations elsewhere in the world.[14]

The contrapuntal interaction between supranationalism and intergovernmentalism has not yet resulted in a victory for either paradigm, although the present trend seems to favour the latter. While federalism still remains an important element of the European integration paradigm, contemporary issues and mood swings in member states as well as the dominance of self-interest have caused some of them to become increasingly sensitive about giving up direct control and veto powers over decision-making. Responding to these forces, the Treaties of Maastricht, Amsterdam and Nice formalised "new techniques of political adaptation that will allow them to remain in charge, at least in formal terms".[15] The European Council has now become an intergovernmental forum which "steers all politically important process by consensus"[16] rather than legislative coordination. Almost predictably, the new draft constitution, which intended to put the enlarged EU more firmly on the federal path, failed to get public or government support in important member countries like France, the Netherlands and the United Kingdom, while some others are still hovering on the sidelines. It seems almost certain that it is back to the drawing board for the EU constitution makers.

Be that as it may, the EU integration process has made giant steps forward since the introduction of the ECSC. The depth of

---

13 Ibid. chapter v.
14 See Y. Devyust, *The European Union at the crossroads: The EU's institutional evolution from the Schuman Plan to the European Convention* (Brussels, P.I.E.-Peter Lang, 2003), p. 5.
15 Ibid. p. 29.
16 Ibid.

the Community integration process is confirmed by the fact that various functions, formerly the exclusive domain of member states, are now being dealt with exclusively on the supranational or pan-European level. As foreseen by Monnet, the European integration process has indeed developed incrementally. During this process, supranationalism as well as intergovernmentalism has become part of the methodology. According to O'Neill:
"The weight of evidence ... tend to suggest that the European integration process was indeed an equivocal one: that no single factor or impulse could adequately explain, nor any theoretical model capture, the complex dynamics of the regional process in Europe. For all their variety, the 'syncretists' do share as their fundamental premises the idea that the processes of international change are neither straightforward nor teleologically driven, and that they amount instead to a mixture of impulses, a competition between interests who hold very different perceptions about the objectives and the possibilities for international cooperation. The syncretic approach to European integration has tried to marry together these apparently conflicting impulses within a new paradigm".[17]

African integration, on the other hand, seems to be the captive of an ideology cast in stone, artificially isolated from the mixture of impulses O'Neill refers to. In deference to anachronistic sovereignty principles, the creators and guardians of this process seem to ignore the essential dynamics of international political procedures in a globalised world. For this reason regional institutions in Africa will continue to founder and remain inferior to the European ones.

The principles and objectives of the AU as set out in Article 3 are broadly the same as expounded by the OAU. Apart from the AU echoing the OAU's emphasis on African unity and solidarity, it also reconfirms the OAU's intergovernmentalist approach by placing heavy emphasis on the recognition of the African borders that came into existence with the achievement of independence, non-interference by any member state in the internal affairs of another and respect for national sovereignty and territorial integrity. Statecentrism is, in the sense that national sovereignty is regarded as an immutable, absolute value, currently a dominant feature of African regional politics. This is a serious impediment in the way of integration. While Europe found practical ways to overcome the sovereignty stumbling block, the pol-

---

17 O'Neill, p. 82.

itical will in Africa to move away from the traditional Westphalian model is largely absent. A glaring paradox in African integration is that while the *ubuntu* philosophy underpins African behavioural attitudes, it does not count for much when sovereignty comes into play. The commitment to statecentrism is a very clear and emphatic principle of the grand design for an "invigorated African continent", as proposed by the AU Act. The objectives of the AU as stipulated by Article 3(a) and (c) of the AU Act, namely to achieve greater unity and solidarity between the African states and to accelerate the political and social economic integration of the continent, are difficult to reconcile with the objective of Article 3(b), which is to defend the sovereignty, territorial integrity and independence of member states. Given the restriction imposed by Article 3(b), regional cooperation envisaged by Article 3(a) and (c) can exist only at a strictly intergovernmental level. Norms and principles on good governance, democracy, human rights, etc. are listed in the AU Act not as conditions of membership, but rather as distant objectives. Although Article 4(h) provides for the right of the Union to intervene in a member state in the case of grave circumstances (war crimes, genocide, crimes against humanity, respect for democratic principles, the rule of law and good governance, and unconstitutional changes of government), the post-colonial political leadership in Africa has always shown extreme reluctance to do so.

From a teleological perspective, therefore, the EU comes closest to a regional ideal type in contemporary international politics, while regional integration in Africa (as is the case with similar experiments in North and South America and Asia) is still in an early phase and has a long way to go yet. While regionalism is definitely a prominent feature of African politics, it manifests in practice as cooperative regionalism rather than the integrationist regionalism demonstrated by the EU.

One of NEPAD's recommendations is the establishment of a Peace and Security Council by the AU with a mandate to implement Article 4(h). However, if the lack of success in executing its APRM regime (by 2005 less than half of African states have agreed to be reviewed) is anything to go by, it seems that Africa may not yet be ready to implement a collective security regime. Failure to deal with the many existing conflicts and cases of human rights abuses and bad governance in Africa as well as the pandering to President Robert Mugabe's harmful autocratic regime in Zimbabwe, seriously question the common will in Africa to live by or apply a regime of collective security. Africa's tolerance of repressive regimes and bad government is a far cry from the EU's doctrine of zero tolerance, particularly as demonstrated in the case of Austria's Jörg Haider and the ethnic cleansing in former Yugoslavia. One ray of hope is the AU's emphasis on sustainable economic development through NEPAD and the accelerated political and socio-economic integration of the continent. The Pan-African Parliament (PAP), inaugurated in September 2004, is supposed to bring the AU closer to the people, in other words, to bring about greater democracy. However, the feasibility of this remains to be seen. As Steven Friedman remarked: "It is not difficult to build a case against the parliament. Its members are not directly elected – they are chosen by their governments. So some are not elected at all or are 'chosen' by voters who did not have a free choice. It has no power to legislate and so can only express sentiments in the hope that those who do have the power will listen".[18] Is this another expensive African white elephant? Perhaps it is too early to tell. However, the only way the PAP could develop legitimacy in the eyes of millions of African people being deprived of democratic freedom in their own countries would be to demonstrate that it is not simply a rubber stamp of government policies, but a truly independent supranational organisation.

Structural features of the African Union and the European Union

The AU and the EU are in essence two very different organisations, particularly in terms of scope, level of integration, internal dynamics, power distribution and decision-making procedures. They are the most similar on the structural level, as illustrated in Table 11.

The institutions of the EU evolved from their forerunners in the EEC, Euratom and the ECSC. Some of these institutions – the European Council, the Council and the Committee of Permanent Representatives – are broadly intergovernmental, while the High Authority of the ECSC, the Commission, the Court of Justice and the European Parliament reflect a supranational character.[19] These institutions do not stand in hierarchical relation to one another, as decision-making power is dispersed among them in a very complex way,[20] reflecting the undefined, open-ended relationship between state power and union power. As summed up

---
18 S. Friedman, "Pan-African Parliament will be what its members make of it", *Business Day*, 29 September 2004, p. 12.
19 C. Archer, *The European Union: Structure and process* (London, Continuum, 2000), pp. 22–35. See also McCormick, pp. 9–20.
20 McCormick, p. 88.

TABLE 11 AFRICAN UNION AND EUROPEAN UNION INSTITUTIONS

The African Union	The European Union
Pan-African Parliament	European Parliament
	Committee of Regions
The Assembly of the Union (Heads of State)	The European Council (Heads of State)
The Executive Council (Ministers)	Council of the European Union (Ministers)
The Commission*	European Commission
The Permanent Representatives Committee	Committee of Permanent Representatives (Coreper)
The Court of Justice*	European Court of Justice
African Peer Review Mechanism	The Ombudsman
The Financial Institutions	The Court of Auditors
–	Europol
The African Bank	European Central Bank
	European Investment Bank
The Specialised Technical Committees	
The Economic, Social and Cultural Council	The Economic and Social Committee

*Still to be established.

by Jones, the EU system is not "a smoothly running, elegantly designed machine", but rather "a contraption with many rough and fuzzy edges, consisting of a set of machines with roughly interacting parts designed by many hands, inspired by different ideas, frequently adapted and roughly tuned. The system comprises a network of interdependent institutions, none of which can function … without reference to others".[21]

The AU structure does not reflect the step-by-step formation of the EU, and is by and large a revamped version of the OAU. The fact that it has nine principal organs against the five of the OAU gives it a new appearance, but it remains to be seen whether these innovations will lead to a better performance. The AU structure is decidedly hierarchical, with the Assembly as "the supreme organ of the Union" (Art. 6.2). Moreover, the Assembly's being composed of heads of states epitomises not only the intergovernmental nature of the AU, but also the immature nature of the integration process in Africa. The only AU institutions that reflect a measure of functional integration are the Executive Council and the Specialised Technical Committees, the

---

21 Jones, pp. 105–106.

latter being accountable to the former, which "shall coordinate and take decisions on policies in areas of common interest to Member States" (Art. 13.1). According to Articles 13 and 14, these functions include a wide array of specialised technical and developmental aspects, such as trade, energy, water resources, education, science and technology, social security, health, environmental matters, transport and communications, etc.

Decision-making and voting

In various ways the EU is neither a state nor a typical international organisation, but has features of both. This uniqueness is particularly reflected in the complicated, if not Byzantine decision-making procedures of the organisation. According to McCormick, the "EU decision-making process is complex and occasionally clumsy, and is still in a process of construction .... [T]he EU institutions are caught in a web of competing national interests [with] conflicting forces of intergovernmentalism and supranationalism … pulling each of them in different directions".[22]

Decision-making on EU level is mainly entrusted to the European Commission, the 786-seat popularly elected European Parliament and the Council of the European Union. The rules and procedures for EU decision-making are prescribed in the treaties. Every EU law is based on a specific treaty article, referred to as the "legal basis" of the legislation. Most ubiquitous among the five major EU decision-making bodies is the European Commission, although the final authority rests largely with the Council of the EU acting in close liaison with the European Council and the European Parliament. The European Commission is responsible for initiating laws and policies, with the final decision taken by the Council of Ministers in a complex interaction with the European Parliament. The European Commission is also responsible for overseeing the implementation of laws and policies by the member states. The European Council, consisting of leaders of member states and the president of the European Commission, meets periodically to guide the broad policies and directions of change of the EU. The Court of Justice is responsible for the development of EU law and passing judgment on matters pertaining to the correlation between EU law, national law and EU treaties.[23]

---

22 *Ibid.* p. 88.
23 *Ibid.* pp. 87–88. See also Archer, pp. 39–62.

The main procedures for enacting new EU laws are (a) consultation, (b) assent, and (c) co-decision. Under the *consultation* procedure, the Commission sends proposals to both the Council of the EU and Parliament but it is the Council that officially consults various other institutions in the EU configuration. In all cases Parliament can (a) approve the Commission proposal, (b) reject the proposal, or (c) ask for amendments. The *assent* procedure means that the Council of the EU has to obtain Parliament's assent before certain very important decisions are taken. These areas are the operational procedures and tasks of the European Central Bank, certain international agreements, accession of new member states and the electoral procedures for Parliament. *Co-decision* embodies the sharing of electoral power by the Council of the EU and Parliament on a wide range of aspects (see box 8).

Although the Treaty of Rome approved a system of Qualified Majority Voting (QMV) for some Council decisions, this mechanism was avoided up to the implementation of the Single European Act (SEA) in 1987, as preference was given to decisions by consensus and unanimity in order to avoid divisions. However, as membership increased, unanimity was increasingly difficult to achieve. With the implementation of the SEA and the Maastricht and Amsterdam Treaties, it was soon clear that EU legislation would only be passed if QMV was used. QMV prescribes a system of weighted voting in the Council and is based on the population size of member states. In the EU of 15 members France, Germany, Italy and the United Kingdom were allotted ten votes each; Spain, eight; Belgium, Greece, the Netherlands and Portugal five each; Austria and Sweden four each; Denmark, Finland and Ireland three each; and Luxembourg two. Until 1 May 2004 the minimum number of votes required for a qualified majority was 62 out of 87. Since 1 November 2004 the number of votes each member in the Council of the European Union can cast, is as follows:

Germany, France, Italy and the UK	29
Spain and Poland	27
Netherlands	13
Belgium, Czech Republic, Greece, Hungary, Portugal	12
Austria and Sweden	10
Denmark, Ireland, Lithuania, Slovakia, Finland	7
Cyprus, Estonia, Latvia, Luxembourg, Slovenia	4
Malta	3

Under the present procedure, a qualified majority will be reached if a majority of the votes (or in some cases a two-third

BOX 8   INSTITUTIONAL INTERACTIONS IN THE EUROPEAN UNION'S POLICY PROCESS[24]

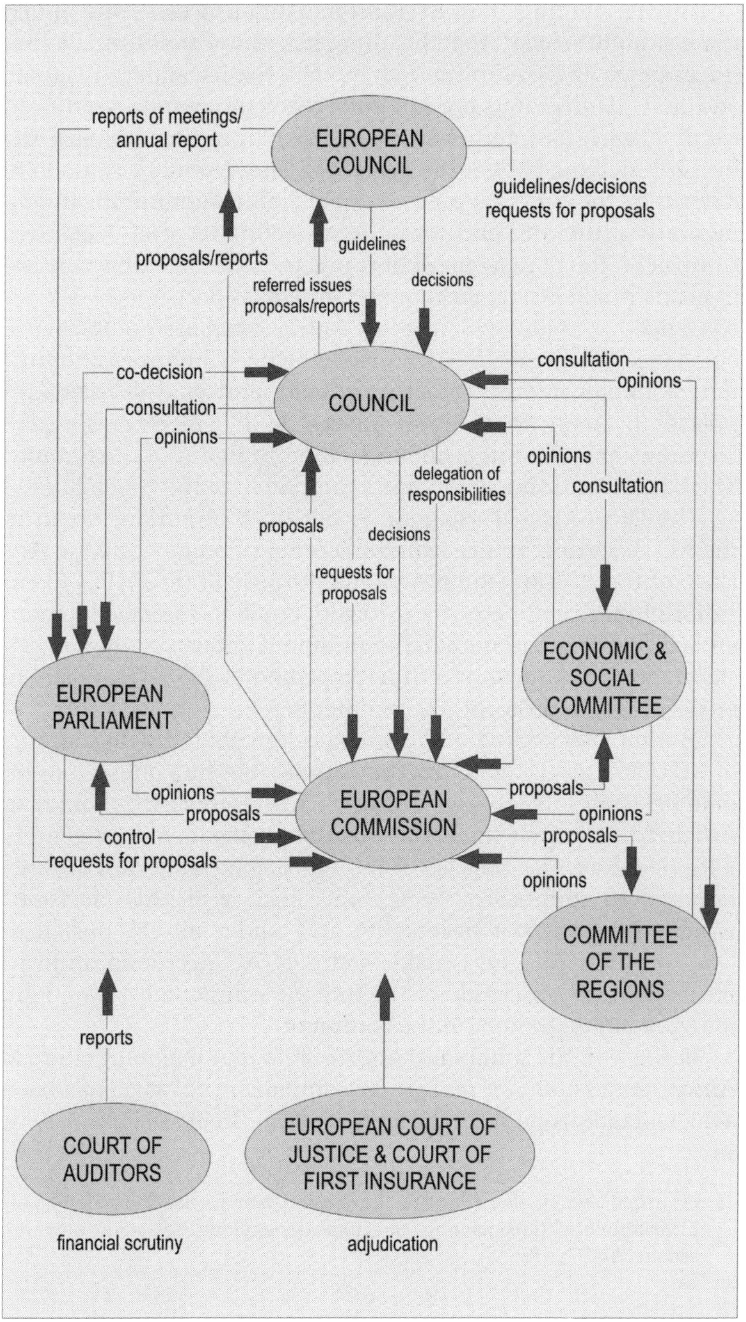

24 Jones, p. 168.

majority) approve, AND if a minimum of 232 votes (73.3%) is cast in favour.[25]

The AU voting and decision-making processes are much more straightforward than EU processes. Important contrasts are the absence of QMV in the AU, the fact that all states are equal, and that AU decisions are not enforceable on member states. In keeping with its intergovernmentalist nature, the primary AU decision-making body is the Assembly. The Assembly is tasked to determine the common policies of the Union, monitor the implementation thereof and provide direction to the Executive Council on the management of conflicts.[26] The Assembly consists of heads of states or governments[27] and takes decisions by way of consensus or, failing which, by a two-thirds majority of the member states.[28] The Executive Council, which is composed of ministers of foreign affairs, "shall coordinate and take decisions on policies in areas of common interest to the member states".[29] Decisions are taken in a similar fashion to that of the Assembly. The Executive Council remains accountable to the Assembly.

The Pan-African Parliament is the third important organ of the AU, according to the sequential order of organs listed in Article 5 of the African Union Act. The purpose of the PAP is to ensure full participation of the African people in the development and economic integration of the continent. However, the composition, powers, functions and organisation of the PAP are still to be defined in a protocol relating thereto.

Nothing is said in the AU's constitution about the legal status of AU decisions, i.e. whether they impose binding obligations on member states. The only indication in this regard is found in Article 23(2), which states that member states failing to comply with decisions and policies of the AU *may* be subjected to sanctions (own emphasis). Non-compliance with AU decisions would therefore not necessarily and under all circumstances lead to sanctions. The variable status of AU decisions confirms once again the strict rule of the intergovernmentalist paradigm in regional integration on the continent.

Because of the minimalist approach to regional integration in Africa, the results are meagre in comparison to what has been achieved in Europe since the signing of the Treaty of Paris in 1951

---

25 European Commission, "How the European Union works: Your guide to the EU institutions" (Luxembourg, Directorate-general for Press and Communications, 2005), p. 19
26 Art. 9.
27 Art. 6.
28 Art. 7.
29 Art. 10.

BOX 9   THE COUNCIL OF THE EUROPEAN UNION'S FUNCTIONAL CONFIGURATIONS AND FUNCTIONS

Different functional configurations of the Council of the EU
- General Affairs and External Relations
- Economic and Financial Affairs
- Justice and Home Affairs
- Employment, Social Policy and Consumer Affairs
- Competitiveness
- Transport, Telecommunications and Energy
- Agriculture and Fisheries
- Environment
- Education, Youth and Culture

Functions of the Council of the EU
- Passing EU laws (some jointly with the European Parliament)
- Coordination of economic policies of member states
- Conclude international agreements
- Approve EU budget
- Develop EU CFSP (following European Council guidelines)
- Coordinate cooperation between the national courts and police forces in criminal matters

BOX 10   FUNCTIONS OF THE EUROPEAN UNION PARLIAMENT

- Power to legislate:
  Shares power with the Council of the EU to legislate.
- Democratic supervision:
  Exercises democratic supervision over all EU institutions, particularly the EU Commission. It has the power to approve or reject nominations of the EU Commissioner and has the right to censure the EU Commission as a whole.
- The power of the purse:
  Shares with the Council authority over the EU budget; influences EU spending; adopts or rejects EU budget in its entirety.

and the introduction of the ECSC. In contrast to the European experience of regional peace and economic prosperity since the introduction of the EEC, the African regional cooperation effort has so far done little in practice to solve the problems of rampant power abuse, human rights violations, bad government, corruption and political and economic decay. The Constitutive Act of the AU and NEPAD took note of these problems, but not much progress has been made beyond aspirational statements.

Of course, it must be noted that an important reason for this discrepancy is that regional integration is invariably a very slow process and that it is perhaps unfair to prejudge the AU on its relative primitiveness in relation to the EU. European regional integration represents a slow step-by-step process, with intellectual roots going back various centuries. In comparison, the pan-African regional integration process is of very recent origin, only starting towards the middle of the 20th century. What is important in the end, however, is that the objectives or rationale of integration are similar in both regions.

An important question is whether it is at all realistic to expect Africa to pursue the EU model. Indeed, according to some of its founding members, the AU was to be modelled after the EU. But it could be a matter of trying to compare cheese and chalk, bearing in mind the uniqueness of both the African and European situations, which seem to prescribe different approaches to regional integration. While superficial similarities between the two organisations do exist, particularly on the structural level, major differences prevail on the functional side, particularly regarding conformity to supranational behavioural attitudes, a priori moral and ethical principles, norms of good governance and democracy, rule making and rule application. But the relatively short existence of regional integration in Africa makes it too early to make a final judgment. The African learning process of the "art of associating together" continues. After all, it took Europe many centuries, many devastating wars and ages of human misery to reach the point where it is now. What should also be borne in mind when comparing the EU and the AU is that regional integration is not a predictable or linear process: it is actually a mixture of many things as it adapts to the unique circumstances of the environment where it takes place. Moreover, from a theoretical point of view, there is no generally accepted "essentialist" definition of integration; it is not a universal or conclusive phenomenon, but "much more a process of becoming than a clear outcome or a definitive political end state".[30]

---

30 O'Neill, p. 1. See also Haas, pp. 10–11.

The sui generis nature of the European Union

When trying to make a comparison between the EU and the AU, it is important to bear in mind that the EU is not a conventional state or an established type of regional organisation; it is, more correctly, a *sui generis* organisation.[31] It is therefore not easy to conceptualise the EU in order to establish a basis for comparison. The first difficulty is that the EU itself is very vague in defining its own political character. The closest it has come is the description in the Maastricht Treaty, Article 1 (formerly Article A) of the Common Provisions (revised by the Amsterdam Treaty), which states: "This Treaty marks a new state in the process of creating an ever closer union among the peoples of Europe, in which decisions are taken as openly as possible and as closely as possible to the citizen". Article 6 (formerly Article F) of the TEU states: "The Union is founded on the principles of liberty, democracy, respect for human rights and fundamental freedoms, and the rule of law, principles which are common to the Member States".

Secondly, the constant flux and change in the EU complicates a generalisation about its true nature. As the integration process has deepened and widened over the years, its character has also changed. "Its nature has never settled."[32]

A third difficulty is the EU's uniqueness of having as its base an eclectic integration paradigm, featuring both supranational and intergovernmental characteristics in its mode of governance. The EU is furthermore a hugely complex and multi-facetted system. "This means that abundant opportunities for different characteristics of the system to be generated by different focus of analyses exist."[33] This aspect is particularly emphasised by the way it shares policy responsibilities with different levels of government and different member states and by its dual sectoral and territorial character.[34]

Legal framework: a benchmark of integration

Although some sources maintain that the AU is "modelled after the European Union",[35] the differences between these two or-

---

31 N. Nugent, *The government and politics of the European Union* (London, Macmillan, 1999), p. 492.
32 *Ibid.* p. 493.
33 *Ibid.*
34 *Ibid.*
35 Wikipedia, "Africa Union".

BOX 11   THE FOUR TREATIES ON WHICH THE EUROPEAN UNION IS FOUNDED

- The Treaty establishing the European Coal and Steel Community (ECSC), which was signed on 18 April 1951 in Paris, came into force on 23 July 1952 and expired on 23 July 2002.
- The Treaty establishing the European Economic Community (EEC), which was signed on 25 March 1957 in Rome and came into effect on 1 January 1958.
- The Treaty establishing the European Atomic Energy Community (Euratom), which was signed in Rome along with the EEC Treaty. These two treaties are generally referred to as the "Treaties of Rome".
- The Treaty of the European Union (TEU), which was signed in Maastricht on 7 February 1992 and came into effect on 1 November 1993.

These treaties have been amended each time new member states have joined:
- The Single European Act (SEA) was signed in February 1986 and was implemented on 1 July 1987. It amended the EEC Treaty and paved the way for completing the single market in the European Community.
- The Treaty of Amsterdam was signed on 2 October 1997 and came into force on 1 May 1999. It amended the EU and EC treaties.
- The Treaty of Nice, signed on 26 February 2001 and coming into force on 1 February 2003, paved the way for the new wave of states that joined the EU in 2004.

ganisations are quite profound. The main reason for these differences is to be found in the different regional paradigms on which these organisations are based: the AU functions like a confederal (intergovernmental) commonwealth of nations, while the EU represents a complicated mix of confederalism and federalism (supranationalism). The practical implications of these different approaches on the all-round functioning of the two organisations are very obvious, but are especially apparent in their legal structures. Apart from some superficial similarities, particularly in the structural domain, a legal comparison therefore highlights the fact that the EU and the AU are two very different political phenomena.

The European Union legal framework

The EU is neither a state nor an international organisation in which member countries voluntarily cooperate without ceding national sovereignty (as with the UN). The organisation is underpinned by its own legal order: it is not merely a creation of law but also pursues its objectives purely by means of law. What makes it unique (compared to other multilateral organisations) is that member countries have voluntarily ceded to the EU the right to act independently and in doing so to establish a common policy across a broad range of important public sectors. The scope and applicability of the EU legal system is both expansive and comprehensive: it has established its own enforceable legal framework, incorporating its own rule-making and rule-adjudication mechanisms; EU law also constitutes an autonomous legal order imposing rights and obligations on both member countries and individuals and limiting the sovereignty of member countries. Therefore the legal system "constitutes a central element of the supranational character of the EU. This has necessarily involved the Member States in surrendering some of their sovereignty, since they are obliged to submit to a legal system over which they have only partial control, and as a corollary their governments are sometimes prevented from introducing national laws they themselves desire".[36] As formulated by the European Court of Justice (Case 6/64, Costa v. ENEL): "By creating a Community of unlimited duration, having its own institutions, its own personality, its own legal capacity of representation on the international plane and, more particularly, real powers stemming from limitation of sovereignty or a transfer of powers from the state to the Community, the Member States have limited their sovereign rights, albeit within limited fields, and have thus created a body of law which binds both their individuals and themselves".[37] It is important to note that contrary to the AU, action regarding tasks assigned to the Community and the direction of the integration process were intentionally not left in the hands of the member states or to the devices of intergovernmentalism. Special Community institutions were created to guide and adjudicate the unification process. The main actors are the European Council, the European Parliament, the Council of Ministers, the Commission, the Court of Justice and the Court of Auditors. Particularly the Court of Justice plays a pivotal role in the judicial process insofar it must ensure that the law is observed in the interpretation and application of the treaties and

---

36 Nugent, p. 276.
37 Ibid. p. 278

the instruments endorsed by them. Under Articles 226 and 227 of the TEC, the Court rules on whether member states have failed to fulfil treaty obligations. In discharging its role and functions, the Court "has successfully defined the principles on which the Community legal order rests, thereby providing the process of European integration with a firm foundation".[38]

The sources of the EU legal order (also referred to as Community law) are found in treaties, legislation, judicial interpretation, international law, customary law, the general principles of law, and conventions between member states. This legal order lays down the procedure for decision-making by the Community institutions and regulates their mutual relationships.

Treaties as source of Community law

The founding treaties, mainly the SEA, the Maastricht Treaty and the Treaty of Amsterdam, as amended over the years, contain the primary legislation of the Community, namely the basic provisions on its objectives, organisation, functions and most of its economic law.

Secondary legislation as source of Community law

Laws adopted by EU institutions constitute the body of "secondary legislation". These laws are concerned with translating the general principles of the treaties into specific rules and are adopted by the Council, by the European Parliament and the Council, or by the Commission, according to prescribed procedures. The treaties distinguish between various kinds of legislation, namely regulations, directives, decisions, recommendations and opinions.

Regulations and general decisions

The legal acts that enable the Community to encroach the furthest on domestic legal systems are in the EC and Euratom Treaties and general decisions in the ECSC Treaty. Two features are of particular importance: their community character and their direct applicability. Community character means that the same laws are laid down throughout the Community, regardless of national borders, and they apply in full to all member states.

---

38 K-D. Borchardt, *The ABC of Community law* (Luxembourg, Office of the Official Publications of the European Communities, 1994), p. 27.

Direct applicability refers to the fact that these laws do not have to be converted into national laws and apply to the Community citizen in the same way as domestic law. The member states and their governing institutions and courts are bound directly by Community law and have to comply with domestic law.[39]

Individual decisions

The individual decision is the means normally available to the Community institutions to order that something is done in an individual case. According to Article 249 of the TEC, a decision (called an individual decision under the ECSC) "shall be binding in its entirety upon those to whom it is addressed". The Community institutions can thus require a member state or an individual to perform or refrain from some action, or they can confer rights or impose duties on them. Individual decisions are usually of a highly specific nature and are adopted in a wide range of circumstances, mostly administrative and technical, like competition policy, to authorise grants from EU funds or to act against dumping.[40]

Directives

According to Article 249 of the TEC, a directive "shall be binding, as to the result to be achieved, upon each Member State to which it is addressed, but shall leave it to the national authorities the choice of form and methods". The reasoning behind directives as a form of legislation is that it allows milder intervention in domestic economic and legal structures. Directives are more general than regulations. Member states can, therefore, consider special domestic circumstances when implementing Community rules. In practice, directives do not supersede the law of the member state, but they do place the member state under an obligation to adapt its national law to Community rules. The assessment of whether it has done so properly is made in the light of Community criteria. "The general principle is that a legal situation must be generated in which the rights and obligations flowing from the directive can be recognized with adequate clarity and certainty so that the Community citizen can rely on them or challenge them, as the case may be, in national courts".[41]

---

39 *Ibid*. pp. 35–36.
40 *Ibid*. p. 246.
41 Borchardt, pp. 37–38.

Recommendations and opinions

This category of law enables the Community institutions to express a view to member states, and in some cases to individual citizens, which is not binding and without legal obligation. It may serve the purpose to float ideas, starting a legislative process, promoting coordination, and encouraging harmonisation.[42] The real significance of the recommendations is political and moral in the sense that those concerned would voluntarily comply with them, which has the indirect legal effect that in the case of non-compliance mandatory instruments may subsequently be passed.

The Community's international agreements as a source of European Union law

As an international role player, the EU is involved in a network of relations with the outside world. As such it must enter into agreements in international law with non-member countries and with other international organisations. These agreements focus particularly on (a) international trade and economic and financial cooperation with developing countries; (b) the establishment of "association agreements" bringing about a special kind of relationship with non-member countries (particularly former European colonies) that goes beyond the mere regulation of trade and involves close economic cooperation and financial assistance; and (c) arrangements to prepare countries for possible membership of the EU or for the establishment of a customs union (Malta in 1971 and Cyprus in 1973).

African Union legal framework

The AU was established through the instrumentality of a "Constitutive Act" adopted by the heads of state and government of its member states on 9 July 2002 in Durban, South Africa. The Constitutive Act of the African Union, later ratified by national parliaments, subsequently became a part of national legal systems.

Noteworthy principles, enumerated in Article 4 of this Act, include the following (see box 7 for more detail):
- Sovereign equality and independence among member states of the Union

---

42 Nugent, p. 247.

- Non-interference by any member state in the internal affairs of another
- The right of the Union to intervene in a member state pursuant to a decision of the Assembly under grave circumstances, such as war crimes, genocide and crimes against humanity
- Respect of borders existing on the achievement of independence
- Establishment of a common defence policy for the African continent
- Prohibition of the use of force or the threat to use force among member states of the Union
- Respect for the sanctity of human life, condemnation and rejection of impunity and political acts of terrorism and subversive activities
- Condemnation and rejection of unconstitutional changes of government.

The Assembly, the supreme organ of the AU, consists of heads of state and government and sets the common policy for the AU. According to Article 7, "[t]he Assembly shall take its decisions by consensus or, failing which, by a two-third majority of the Member States of the Union". A simple majority decides procedural matters, including the question whether or not a matter is procedural. Whereas the EU member states have limited their legislative sovereignty and in so doing have created an autonomous body of law that is binding to them and their nationals, the AU has no such legal authority. Unless consensus or a two-third majority is obtained in the Assembly on a specific issue, each member state of the AU can interpret the provisions of the Constitutive Act in its own way and decide individually in what way the objectives of the Act will be maximized.

Article 23 provides for the imposition of appropriate sanctions, to be determined by the Assembly, against non-complying member states. The Assembly is empowered to determine appropriate sanctions to be enforced on a member state that defaults in the payment of its contributions to the AU budget. Such sanctions include denial of the right to speak at meetings, to vote, to present candidates for any position or post in the AU, or to benefit from any AU activity or commitment. Furthermore, any member state that fails to comply with AU decisions or policies *may* (own emphasis) be subjected to other sanctions such as the denial of transport and communication links with other member states as well as political and economic measures to be determined by the Assembly. Governments that have come to power through unconstitutional means will not be allowed to participate in activities of the AU.[43]

The Court of Justice (still to be established) "shall be seized with matters of interpretation" arising from the application or implementation of the Constitutive Act. This court is not to be confused with the African Court on Human and Peoples' Rights. The latter was established by the Protocol to the African Charter on Human and Peoples' Rights, which was adopted in 1998 and entered into force in January 2005. Existing regional instruments that established European and Inter-American Courts inspired the Court of Justice. The Assembly decided at its Third Ordinary Session, held in Addis Ababa in July 2004 that the Court of Justice and the African Court on Human and People's Rights should be integrated. It requested that the chairperson of the Commission of the AU work out the modalities of implementing this decision and then submit a report to the next Ordinary Session. The jurisdiction of the Court of Justice extends to all cases and disputes submitted to it concerning the interpretation and application of the Charter on Human and Peoples' Rights (Bajul Charter), the Protocol and any other relevant human rights instrument ratified by the states concerned. By extending this jurisdiction, the Court is able to make a decision based on these instruments that may include the award of reparations or other remedies where the Court finds a violation. The Court may also render advisory opinions at the request of a member state.[44] In terms of Article 2 of the Protocol, the Court has the mandate to complement and reinforce the functions of the African Commission on Human and Peoples' Rights, which was established to promote and protect human and peoples' rights in Africa.[45]

Economic integration

As is the case with legal integration, levels of economic integration in the EU and Africa are probably too far apart to deserve comparison. Since the signing of the ECSC Treaty, economic integration has been the *sine qua non* of European integration and has developed into a sophisticated, systematic and comprehensive system of regional integration.

In spite of the extreme urgency of its economic agenda, Africa lags far behind. The SADC, which many hold as the hope and

---

43 Constitutive Act of the African Union, Art. 30, signed in Lomé, July 2000.
44 Art. 4 of the Constitutive Act.
45 C. E. Welch, "The African Commission on Human and Peoples' Rights: A five year report and assessment", *Human Rights Quarterly*, 14 (1992), p. 43.

locomotive for economic recovery and growth in a Southern African region where the vast majority of people still live in abject poverty, is allowed to languish in virtual dysfunctional disarray because of a lack of leadership and direction, and bureaucratic ineptness. Market integration is seen as the key driver of regional integration, but movement is glacial and deadlines come and go as member states follow their own agendas. A free trade area is envisioned for 2008, a customs union for 2010, a common market for 2015, and a single currency for 2018.[46] Given the urgent nature of the problems at hand, these time scales are unacceptably slow. Although eurosclehrosis also hampered the EU progress at critical times, it was overcome by good leadership and purpose in its various institutions. Therefore, the European experience and methodology on getting things done and proceeding with the agenda should be looked at in order to make a greater success of the faltering African regional experiment.

Until the introduction of NEPAD (see Chapter 8 for more information on NEPAD), the AU, as was the case with its predecessor, the OAU, was largely driven by political goals. Economics, although recognised as an important problem, took the backseat to Africa's political, strategic and diplomatic goals. European integration, on the other hand, was largely motivated and driven by economic and security considerations. With the establishment of NEPAD economic and developmental issues were prioritised, but no meaningful results are visible yet. An important disadvantage of NEPAD, in contrast to EU economic integration processes and mechanisms, is that it is based on intergovernmental cooperation rather than regional supranationalism. The same applies to African sub-regional organisations like the SADC and the Economic Community of West African States (ECOWAS), where statecentrism dominates the decision-making processes and where very few successes in the economic field have been registered so far. Supranationalism and functionalism, as introduced by the ECSC at the beginning of the EU integration process, do not yet exist in the AU or sub-regional African regionalization vocabulary. While African integration (continental and sub-continental) continues to focus on grand designs or the "one size fits all" syndrome, the European model follows a gradualist tactic. It goes without saying that the latter approach to regional engineering has been the more successful one.

Regionalism aimed at the promotion of economic growth in sub-Saharan Africa has become more salient because of two factors in particular, the first of which was South Africa's emergence

---

46 This is according to the South African Deputy Foreign Minister, Aziz Pahad, cited in *Business Day*, 18 August 2006.

from isolation to become a regional role player. As pointed out by Jenkins and Thomas, part of the reason for the failure of African regional groupings is due to the "lack of a large, more developed partner to provide both a significant regional market and a source of external capital and expertise."[47] South Africa, as the continent's largest economy (producing about 25% of total African GDP and 70% of the SADC's GDP), filled this gap in the SADC regional configuration. The second factor was growing fears in recent years that Africa was facing marginalization. The enlargement of the EU from 15 to 25 members and the new dynamics in the integration between North and South America "created the perception that Africa risks being left behind in the formation of regional economic blocs, with adverse consequences for trade and investment."[48]

Apart from the SADC and SACU, various other regional bodies that focus mainly on economic cooperation exist on the African continent. These are mainly the Common Market of Eastern and Southern Africa (COMESA), the Cross-Border Initiative (CBI), the Common Monetary Area (CMA), Communité Economique de l'Afrique de l'Ouest (CEAO), Union Doaunière et Economique de l'Afrique Centrale (UDEAC), and ECOWAS. Apart from their economic focus, an important feature of these regional bodies is their overlapping membership and the "confusing picture of priorities"[49] they present. These regional bodies are supposed to be building blocks for NEPAD, although the possibility does exist that their role and importance will be downgraded or even diminish following the strong new emphasis by African political leaders, the G7 and the EU on NEPAD as the answer to Africa's economic woes.

While the jury is still out on the efficacy of NEPAD, and considering the fact that most of the above mentioned sub-regional bodies are generally unsuccessful in their quest to develop and modernise the African economy, it is unlikely that the wide quantitative and qualitative gap between EU and African economic integration will narrow. This discrepancy is particularly highlighted by a comparison between the monumental concrete achievements of economic integration in Europe since the finalisation of the Treaty of Rome in 1957 and Africa's poor track record. From this point of view, it is a great pity that NEPAD was not created along similar lines as the ECSC and the underlying principles and goals of the Treaty of Rome.

---

47 Jenkins & Thomas, p. 153.
48 Ibid. p. 153.
49 Ibid. p. 154.

Achievements of European Union economic and functional integration

It is instructive to use the EU's performance as a benchmark of what could be possible under an authentic supranational model of integration for the African economy. The three primary goals of the Treaty of Rome underline the priority given to economic integration in Europe. The first was the creation of a European customs union that brought about the removal of all tariff barriers and other obstacles to trade among the EEC members, an agreement on a common external tariff and a common commercial policy towards other countries. A second major goal was the creation of a European common market, which would allow the free movement of people, goods, services and money among Community members. For this purpose EEC members had to approve a common rule to avoid economic distortions, leading to the development of a common competition policy, the eradication of monopolies and cartels and the harmonisation of national health and safety standards. Thirdly, EEC members agreed to develop a common agricultural policy aimed at ensuring that farmers were paid guaranteed prices for their produce, that food supplies were secured and that markets were stabilised.[50] Of these three objectives the customs union proved the least problematic and an agreement was reached on a common external tariff in 1988. It was only in the face of the threat of economic decline and recession in the 1970s, as well as serious competition from American and Japanese high technology industries, that EEC members finally changed their conservative thinking on supranational cooperation. They agreed on the SEA, reforms to the CAP and, to bring about exchange rate stability, eventually also to a single European currency.

Although it took the member states a long time to get to this point, their adoption of the SEA in 1987 was a landmark achievement for European integration.[51] The goal of the SEA was to create a Single European Market (SEM), aiming at the removal within five years of the remaining non-tariff barriers to the free movement of people, capital, goods and services between the member states. It also had to enable the EU to act jointly and present a common front in its economic and trading relations with other countries.

---

50 McCormick, p. 175.
51 See A. Moravcsic, "Negotiating the Single European Act: National interests and conventional statecraft in the European Community" in Nelsen & Stubb (eds), pp. 217–240.

These last barriers that had to be eradicated were mainly physical, fiscal and technical. The physical barriers on the movement of people in the form of border control posed serious constraints to economic progress in the Community and on the development of a European identity: it was time-consuming, wasteful and costly. With the signing of the Schengen Agreement by the Benelux countries, France and Germany in 1985, border controls were "fast-tracked". However, it was only fully implemented in 1995 when the Amsterdam Treaty brought it under the umbrella of the EU; the other member states, except the United Kingdom and Ireland, also joined "Schengenland".[52]

Fiscal barriers in the Community, particularly in the form of varying value added tax (VAT) levies and excise duties, put up trade barriers such as unequal competition and artificial price differences. Agreement was reached in 1991 on a minimum VAT rate of 15%, and in 1992 minimum rates for excise duties were also agreed upon in the Community. Since then, agreement has also been reached on a VAT system whereby tax is only collected at a local rate in the country of origin, with the ultimate goal a Community-wide single VAT rate.[53]

Technical barriers, comprised of different safety, health, environmental and consumer protection standards and regulations, were almost insurmountable in the quest for a single market in Europe. However, three important developments helped to remove many bureaucratic and political obstacles: the European Court's Cassis de Dijon decision in 1979 on the principle of recognition of local produce; the 1983 mutual information directive requiring member states to inform the Commission and other member states of their intention to introduce new domestic technical regulations, and allow them three months to respond if they felt these would create new barriers to intra-Community trade produce; and the Cockfield report, which paved the way for the Council of Ministers to agree on new laws, with objectives and detailed specifications to be drawn up by existing private institutions such as the European Standardisation Committee and the European Electrotechnical Standardisation Committee.

The impact of the single market on the EC economy was profound and even radical. Barring only minor restrictions, any resident of the Community can now live and work in all other member states; the European transport, energy and telecommunication systems were revitalised and modernised; regulations on air transport were relaxed, resulting in open skies over Europe,

---
52 McCormick, pp. 176–178.
53 *Ibid.* pp. 178–179.

cheaper airfares and the privatisation and merger of airlines; and the broadcasting and film industries and telecommunication systems were wrested from American domination and became more "Europeanised".

The single market in Europe signified agreement among members on economic policies, but the process of economic integration also needed a monetary union. As early as the 1950s European leaders saw stable exchange rates as the essence of bringing about a common market economic union. When the post-war fixed exchange system collapsed in 1971 with the United States' decision to abandon the gold standard, the idea of a monetary union became highly salient. Initially, exchange rate fluctuations were kept under control first by way of linkage to Germany's deutschmark (referred to as the "currency snake"), and afterwards, in 1979, by the European Monetary System (EMS). In order to reduce currency fluctuations relative to each other, economic and fiscal policies were coordinated through an Exchange Rate Mechanism (ERM) based on a European accounting and currency unit (ECU). In the end, however, these arrangements proved imperfect and unsatisfactory. With the completion of the single market and the convergence of views on economic matters by the EC leadership in the mid-1980s, the step-by-step realisation of a European Economic and Monetary Union (EMU) became possible. The final step was taken with the signing of the Maastricht Treaty and its ratification in 1993. Under the terms of the treaty, the exchange rates for the participating countries were irrevocably fixed from 1 January 1999, and a common currency, the euro, was introduced from 1 January 2002. The completion of the EMU is, no doubt, one of the most ambitious steps taken by the EU since the process of integration began with the ECSC.

African Union and European Union security policies and conflict management

Community formation in Europe was preceded by a long history of political intolerance among states, aggressive manifestations of nationalism, rampant militarism and intermittent nationalistic wars. The devastation of World War 2 finally convinced Europeans to mend their ways, to discard their selfish zero-sum driven political behaviour and to embark on a new paradigm of peaceful co-existence through regional cooperation and integration. The success of the new approach, despite a modest beginning with community formation focussing solely on coal and steel at the Treaty of Paris (1951), proved phenomenal as time went by. Not only did interstate conflict stop altogether, but (western) European security and welfare have reached unprecedented heights, and the EU members have grown from 6 to 25 countries.

The European Union's Common Foreign and Security Policy

In world affairs the EU is "an economic giant and political pygmy".[54] Although it is engaged in a significant range of external relationships, it is "still widely regarded as essentially a *civil power*, with an international role primarily concerned with external economic relations .... Its weight in international affairs derives from the economic carrots and sticks at its disposal."[55] This discrepancy between political power and economic power, and the fact that the EU is not punching its weight in world affairs, have much to do with the dominance of statecentrism over supranationalism in the EU. As a result, the EU suffers under a dual foreign policy presence and personality; member states, as a rule, put their own sovereign national interests and objectives above that of the Community.

Apart from the sovereignty issue, EU member states are loath to pool resources under an EU security umbrella because many of them already feel safe enough under existing security arrangements. This refers to the "variable geometry" in Europe's security architecture: a complex network of institutions with overlapping memberships and functions that exist across the European landscape. These are all intergovernmental security bodies that do not threaten the sovereign identity of member states. They include the North Atlantic Treaty Organisation (NATO), the Western European Union (WEU), the Euro-Atlantic Partnership Council (EAPC), the Rapid Reaction Force (RRF) and the Council of Europe (CE), and the Organisation for Security and Cooperation in Europe (OSCE). Moreover, NATO has successfully redesigned its role after the Cold War, played a decisive role in the Balkans, and is viewed by many as the cornerstone of collective security in Europe.

The TEU formally established an intergovernmental CFSP as one of the EU's three pillars. The Treaty required member states "to co-ordinate their action in international organisations and to uphold common positions in international forums ... [and] to

---

54 Jones, p. 430.
55 *Ibid.*

BOX 12 EUROPEAN UNION INVOLVEMENT IN REGIONAL PEACE AND SECURITY INITIATIVES IN AFRICA SINCE 1994[56]

- The EU supported the development of the AU's Mechanism for Conflict Prevention and gave funds in aid of its Peace Fund and early warning system
- The Africa-Europe Summit (Cairo 2002) renewed the commitment of the parties to cooperate in the areas of conflict prevention, management and resolution, and peace building
- In April 2002 a programme in support of the AU peace-building and transition activities was signed. The main purpose was to fund the activities of the Peace and Security Council (€10 million), reinforcing the AU's capacity building in transitional phases (€2 million)
- In November 2003 the EU approved the allocation of €250 million from the EDF for the creation of an African Peace Facility in support of African led operations and to enhance the capacity of African institutions to carry out such operations
- In December 2003 the European Council reiterated its commitment to support peace processes in the Great Lakes, Liberia, Côte d'Ivoire, Sudan, Somalia, Ethiopia and Eritrea
- The EU supported sub-regional efforts by the SADC and ECOWAS for the peaceful settlement of conflicts in Burundi, the Democratic Republic of the Congo and Liberia.

support the Union's external and security policy actively and unreservedly in a spirit of loyalty and mutual solidarity".[57] However, in response to a general acknowledgement that TEU references to the CFSP contained various debilitating lacunae (particularly highlighted by its ineffectiveness in response to the crisis in the Balkans and the predicted implications of future enlargement), the Treaty of Amsterdam (1997) approved various improvements to make it more coherent and with clearer objectives. These include:
- The empowerment of the European Council to frame a common defence policy "which might lead to a common defence" (a decision to be ratified by each member state)

---

56 F. Faria, "Crisis management in sub-Saharan Africa: The role of the European Union", occasional paper no. 51 (Paris, Institute for Security Studies, April 2004).
57 *Ibid.* p. 437.

- The resuscitation of the WEU from its largely moribund status to become, in effect, the military wing of the EU, with the responsibility to draw up and put into practice any defence decisions
- The empowerment of the EU to carry out humanitarian aid and peacekeeping tasks (known as the Petersburg tasks), and to devise common strategies, general policy guidelines, joint actions and common positions
- The establishment of a troika, consisting of the Presidency of the Council, the Commission and a "High Representative" for the CFSP to represent the EU in the European Council
- The provision for greater cooperation between members of the EU in pursuit of a CFSP.

Although the provisions of the Treaty of Amsterdam no doubt improved the capacity of the EU to deal with regional security and to act in international crises, it still left much room for improvement. Progress in this respect was made in December 1998 when the French and British governments issued the St-Malo Declaration, which proclaimed the need for a stronger European defence capability that would enable the Union to act more independently from (although not in opposition to) the NATO United States. Further decisions were taken to beef up the EU's preparedness and capability as actor in European crises by the European Council meetings in Cologne in June 1999 and Helsinki in December 1999 respectively. These resolutions resulted in operational measures for a European Security and Defence Policy (ESDP) and for an EU RRF. Although the ESDP did not replace the defence policies of member states and the RRF is not a European army, the groundwork was laid for the EU to develop a "greater capacity for autonomous action".[58] According to Javier Solana (High Representative of the CFSP), the ESDP should not be seen as a process of militarisation of European construction. It is rather an effort to deal more effectively with an increasingly complex and unpredictable world, to bring greater coherence to the ESS, to find a better balance between European nations and institutions and to maintain a Euro-American relationship in line with changes in the world and in each of the partners of NATO. The aim, according to Solana, is to "promote the Union as a global political player, capable of mobilising all re-

---

58 J-Y. Haine, "An historical perspective" in N. Gnesotto (ed.), *EU Security and Defence Policy: The first five years (1999–2004)* (Paris, Institute for Security Studies, 2004), p. 43.

**BOX 13   OFFICIAL AIMS OF THE COMMON FOREIGN AND
            SECURITY POLICY**[59]

- To safeguard the common values, fundamental interests, independence and integrity of the EU in conformity with the United Nations Charter
- To strengthen the security of the EU in all ways
- To preserve peace and strengthen international security, in accordance with the principles of the United Nations Charter as well as the principles of the Helsinki Final Act and the objectives of the Paris Charter, including those on external borders
- To promote international cooperation
- To develop and consolidate democracy, the rule of law and respect for human rights and fundamental freedoms

sources available – economic, commercial, humanitarian, diplomatic and, of course, military – to act in a coherent and above all effective manner over the whole of its international environment". He articulates the strategic principles of the ESDP as follows: "[to] develop a greater degree of international justice and respect for law; build patiently the minimum conditions for good governance and democracy; favour negotiation rather than conflict, but agree to intervene and coerce when coercion becomes necessary".[60]

Although a collective European approach to defence and security policy has always been a difficult and elusive policy target, good progress has been made since the Kosovo wake-up call. The various steps taken in the last five years have now put the EU in the position to assume direct responsibility for crisis management, to have a military staff, to take responsibility for military operations, to act in unison in the event of a terrorist attack, and to work on the basis of a "genuinely European security strategy".[61] However, while a basis now exists for better cooperation in the context of the CFSP, the depth and scope of genuine regional integration has not improved a great deal from a qualitative perspective. The CFSP is still essentially an intergovernmental arrangement. Moreover, being the product of so many compromises among member states, it has all the characteristics and

---

59 S. P. McGiffen, *The European Union: A critical guide* (London, Pluto, 2001), p. 50.
60 Solana, "Preface" in Gnesotto (ed.), pp. 6, 10.
61 Solana, "Preface", p. 5.

BOX 14 MAIN FEATURES OF THE EUROPEAN SECURITY AND DEFENCE POLICY[62]

- It will give the EU a crisis management and conflict prevention capability
- It absorbs the WEU's crisis management and conflict prevention tasks
- It establishes new political and military structures for EU security and defence
- A 60 000 strong EU RRF (introduced by 2003)
- The RRF is not a European army and contributing states decide on their own deployments
- RRF operations intend to draw on NATO assets and capabilities
- It is viewed as complementary to NATO, not as an opponent
- Other countries may be invited to participate in ESDP operations.

dangers of a bureaucratic labyrinth. Its machinery is complicated and cumbersome. It has too many "faces" (the Council Presidency and the High Representative, then the commissioner for external relations and the foreign ministers of member states) and over-elaborate procedures, while conflicts over objectives and resource allocations could stymie future cooperation and progress.[63]

Structures alone are not sufficient to ensure success for the CFSP pillar of the EU. For real and lasting success in the future much depends on the existence of a common political will and leadership. The negative responses by France, the Netherlands and the United Kingdom to the new constitutional proposals to guide the EU into the future, the divisions over the war in Iraq and conflicting views on the role of the United States in the European security equation are indications of a house still divided and a bumpy road lying ahead for the CFSP.

Regional integration and African security

In Africa we find a different, if not reverse pattern to the one that characterises conflict history and conflict regulation in Europe. Before colonial annexation, sub-Saharan Africa was a relatively

---

62 Jones, p. 455.
63 Jones, p. 461.

peaceful entity,[64] a vast geographical landmass without states and without national borders. Colonialism significantly changed that. The tribal based geopolitical configuration and the generally peaceful nature of the African political process made way for the creation of weak, mostly dysfunctional states (many of them deeply divided along ethnic lines), the emergence of a new political and military elite, and the replacement of traditional consensus-seeking politics with a zero-sum, adversarial political style. The seeds of conflict-driven politics were planted by legitimate liberation struggles, mostly through guerrilla warfare, in various African states during the last phases of colonialism. Eventually these struggles together with changes in international public opinion brought colonialism to an end by the middle of the 20th century. The anti-colonial guerrilla struggles precipitated a future scenario characterised by ethnic intolerance, political power struggles, militarism, and economic decay in many of the newly independent African states. Military *coups d'état* and brutal civil wars spread like wild fires in these states. "Africa's post-colonial history has tended to be one of poor governance, authoritarianism, corruption, exploitation of state wealth for the enrichment of elites, and failed or dysfunctional states."[65]

Under these circumstances political order, economic development and modernization has been extremely difficult, if not impossible goals for the newly independent states on the African continent. After the passage of more than half a century, these obstacles are yet to have been overcome. In some cases they have even deteriorated over the years, affecting the security environment essential for creating better life conditions for the long-suffering African masses. A conspicuous paradox of African politics is that despite the glorification of African unity and African fraternity by the leadership elite, ethnic conflict, civil war and power struggles have become a regular pattern of political behaviour in many countries. Most African leaders have exercised power in an anarchic Hobbesian way, subjecting democratic principles, the rule of law and good governance to the whims of their political power and military might. African unity has become the slogan and rallying cry of the powerful and the elite, but a meaningless political doctrine for the suffering masses. Another paradox is that massive aid support by the former colonial powers in order to develop and stabilise their former colon-

---

64 This is with the rare exception of the warlike Zulu nation under the leadership of Shaka and Dingaan in the early 19th century.
65 E. Sidiripoulos (ed.), *A continent apart: Kosovo, Africa and humanitarian intervention* (Johannesburg, South African Institute for International Affairs, 2001), p. xvi.

ies has had only the opposite effect in most cases. And in spite of a plethora of initiatives and plans by Africa itself, the United Nations, the World Bank and the IMF to guide Africa to peace, development and prosperity, the status quo of conflict, underdevelopment, poor governance, authoritarianism and economic decay have as yet not been altered in any meaningful way.

African leaders, African intelligentsia and foreign role players and interested parties alike regard regional integration as an important precondition for peace and progress in Africa. In fact, after decolonisation, a plethora of defence and security related instruments have been established at a continental level (see box 16). Many of these were poorly managed ad hoc responses without teeth on the implementation side and lacking coherence;[66] others amounted to window dressing with little or no practical consequence. Until the Sirte (Libya) meeting of the AU on 28 February 2004, African nations had no overarching formal policy on how to deal with conflict on the continent. The results were tragic, epitomised by an estimated half a million people who died in the genocide in Rwanda in 1994 while the AU's predecessor, the OAU, did nothing. During its inaugural summit in Durban in July 2002, the AU initiated the formulation of a Common African Defence and Security Policy (CADSP) in line with the objectives of its Constitutive Act (Article 3(a) to (h) and Article 4 (d)). According to the draft framework proposed by the African ministers of defence and security in Addis Ababa on 20 and 21 January 2004: "The adoption of a Common Defence and Security Policy for Africa is premised on a common African perception of what is required to be done collectively by African states to ensure that Africa's common defence and security interests and goals ... are safeguarded in the face of common threats to the continent as a whole." The AU Heads of State and Government meeting in Sirte duly approved this proposal. In a Solemn Declaration on a Common African Defence and Security Policy they declared their "commitment to uphold and give practical expression" to it. The declaration is interspersed with references to unity and cooperation among African states. Specific references are made to:
- The "continental character" of the CADSP
- A "common understanding" among African nations as to what the CADSP stands for
- The "indivisibility" of African security on the harmonization of member states' defence and security activities

---

66 A. Mohammed, P. Tesfagioris & A. de Waal, "Peace and security dimensions of the African Union", ad hoc background paper for AFD 111 (Addis Ababa, Economic Commission for Africa, 2001).

- Consultation among member states to adopt a common position on matters relating to defence that affect or constitute a potential threat to the collective security of Africa
- Collective responses to both internal and external threats
- Eliminating suspicions and rivalry among African states
- Providing a framework for AU member states to cooperate in defence matters
- Advancing the cause of integration in Africa
- The promotion of a culture of peace and peaceful co-existence among AU member states.[67]

However, all these references to unity and cooperation stop well short of committing the AU to supranationalism. Like the EU's CFSP, the CADSP is essentially an expression of intergovernmental or statecentric cooperation and not regional integration *per se*. Africa has also not yet advanced to the status of pluralistic "security community", in the Deutschian sense of the word, by being a lesser form of integration.[68] Its ruling paradigm is firmly based on "sovereign equality" and "non-interference by any Member State in the internal affairs of others".[69] Article 4 of the Constitutive Act of the AU does, however, give the Union the right to "intervene in a Member State pursuant to a decision by the Assembly [of the AU], in respect of grave circumstances, namely: war crimes, genocide and crimes against humanity, as well as a serious threat to legitimate order, in order to restore peace and stability to the Member States of the Union, upon the recommendation of the Peace and Security Council [of the AU]." Similar to the EU's CFSP, the CADSP puts the emphasis on dealing with both traditional military aggression and socio-economic causes of conflict. Accordingly, it proclaims: "The causes of intra-state conflict necessitate a new emphasis on human security, based not only on political values but on social and economic imperatives as well. This new multi-dimensional notion of security thus embraces such issues as human rights; the right to participate fully in the process of governance; the right to equal development, as well as the right to have access to resources and the basic necessities of life; the right to protection against poverty; the right to conducive education; the right to protection against marginalization on the basis of gender; protection against natural disasters, as well as ecological and environmental degradation".[70]

---

67 Declaration on a Common African Defence and Security Policy, (Sirte, Libya, 28 February 2004), chapter 111.
68 *Ibid*.
69 *Ibid*.
70 *Ibid*.

BOX 15   PRINCIPLES AND VALUES UNDERLYING THE COMMON AFRICAN DEFENCE AND SECURITY POLICY[71]

- Sovereign equality and interdependence among member states
- Respect of borders existing on achievement of independence
- Peaceful resolution of conflicts among member states
- Prohibition of the use of force, or threat of use of force among member states
- Non-interference by any member state in the internal affairs of another
- The right of the AU to intervene in a member state in grave circumstances, namely war crimes, genocide, crimes against humanity and a serious threat to legitimate order, in order to restore peace and stability to the member states, upon the recommendation of the Peace and Security Council
- Peaceful co-existence of member states and their right to live in peace and security
- The right of member states to request intervention from the Union in order to secure peace and security
- Promotion of self-reliance within the framework of the Union
- Respect for democratic principles, human rights, the rule of law and good governance
- Promotion of social justice to ensure balanced economic development
- Respect for the sanctity of human life and condemnation and rejection of impunity and political assassination, acts of terrorism and subversive activities
- Condemnation and rejection of unconstitutional changes of governments
- Restraint by any member state from entering into any treaty or alliance that is incompatible with the principles and objectives of the Union
- Prohibition of any member state from allowing the use of its territory as a base for aggression and subversion against any member state
- Promotion of gender equality.

71   Ibid.

Unquestionably, if the above goals were pursued with the same commitment and rigour in Africa as is the case in the EU, many of the obstacles still in the way of an African Renaissance would be overcome. Unfortunately, however, the chasm between aspirational declarations and reality in Africa remains far too wide. At the same time, the threshold for intervention is very high and it is mostly in prima facie cases (after most of the damage has already been done, in any case) such as Burundi and Darfur, where the AU does step in.[72] The AU Assembly, the supreme decision-making body of the CADSP, is an interstate body, and in spite of the strong emphasis on cooperation and collective action referred to above, AU member states are traditionally extremely loath to interfere in each other's affairs. So far only about half of the African states have subscribed to NEPAD's APRM, no finger has been lifted to stop human rights violations in Zimbabwe and virtual anarchy in the Côte d'Ivoire and the Democratic Republic of the Congo continue to challenge the AU's commitment to the peace and security regime agreed to at Sirte.

Apart from the lack of political will and commitment among its members and the reality of the imperative of the non-intervention principle being stronger than the "non-indifference" principle, the AU does not have the resources to effectively resolve conflict in the African region. In fact, in most cases it has to rely on outside support by the United Nations and foreign powers and on donor assistance. The CADSP is certainly an important step forward for peace and security in Africa, but at this stage its ambitions do not match its power and efficiency as an instrument of peace and security.

Conclusion

So far, EU and South African efforts to promote regional integration in Africa show little in terms of substantive results. Both the EU and South Africa seem to ignore or abide by the debilitating political culture that underpins African regionalism. Both should probably know better. They allow the mantra of African unity and an anachronistic interpretation of the sovereignty principle to continue to provide a protective shield for wayward regimes and leaders. While it is diplomatically prudent to wait for the democratic processes in the countries suffering under corrupt regimes to set upon a self-correcting course, as South Africa and

---

72 The crisis in Darfur was depicted by the UN "as the worst humanitarian and human rights catastrophe in the world".

BOX 16 AFRICAN POST-COLONIAL CONTINENTAL DEFENCE AND SECURITY RELATED INSTRUMENTS AND MECHANISMS

- The Constitutive Act of the AU
- AU Peace and Security Protocol
- African Standby Force
- The Convention for the Elimination of Mercenaries in Africa
- African Nuclear-Weapon-Free Zone Treaty
- The Bamako Convention on the ban of the Import of and control of Trans-boundary Hazardous Wastes into Africa
- The Bamako Declaration on an African Common Position on the Illicit Proliferation, Circulation, and Trafficking of Small Arms and Light Weapons
- The Algiers Convention on the Prevention and Combating of Terrorism, and the Algiers Plan
- The Kempton Park Plan of Action on a Landmine-Free Africa
- The African Charter on Human and Peoples' Rights
- The Protocol to the African Charter on Human and Peoples' Rights on the Establishment of an African Court on Human and Peoples' Rights
- The African Charter on the Rights and Welfare of the Child
- The Declaration of the Assembly of Heads of State and Government of the OAU on the Political and Socio-economic Situation in Africa and the Fundamental Changes Taking Place in the World
- The Declaration of the Assembly of the Heads of State and Government on the Establishment within the OAU of a Mechanism for Conflict Prevention, Management and Resolution
- The Grand Bay (Mauritius) Declaration and Plan of Action
- The Declaration on the Framework for a Response to Unconstitutional Changes of Government
- The Declaration and Plan of Action on Drug Abuse and Illicit Trafficking Control in Africa
- The Abuja Declaration on HIV/AIDS, Tuberculosis and Other Related Infectious Diseases
- The Abuja Declaration on Roll Back Malaria in Africa
- Declaration on the Code of Conduct on International Relations
- The 1969 OAU Convention Governing Specific Aspects of Refugee Problems in Africa
- The Cairo Agenda for Action
- The African Charter for Popular Participation in Development
- Instruments on the Rights of Women
- The Conference on Security, Stability, Development and Cooperation in Africa
- New Economic Partnership for African Development

the EU seem to do, the question of moral responsibility remains unanswered. South Africa's newfound liberty and democracy seem to have little or no impact on its foreign policy towards faltering regimes in Africa. While the EU is effective in compelling its own members to abide by a common code of morality, political responsibility and economic discipline, the same regimen is not applied in Africa in spite of the norms laid down by the AU Constitutive Act and the existence of an African Commission on Human and Peoples' Rights. The reluctance or inability of the EU and South Africa to deal more competently with African governments who so utterly and continuously fail to meet civilised standards of human rights contradict the ideals they pursue domestically. Although Rome was not built in a day, regional bodies should be systematically empowered with the necessary legal authority to augment national systems or even to override the national sovereignty of member states on matters of common concern, particularly in the field of human rights, democracy and the rule of law. This way African integration would become an instrument of continental development and stability.

As discussed earlier, compared to the EU model, African regional integration is a very limited arrangement. It does not go beyond straightforward intergovernmental cooperation. A lone voice to introduce supranationalism came from Libya's Colonel Muammar al-Qaddafi when he introduced his vision for a "United States of Africa", with a single army, currency, and an AU chairman with presidential powers to the African heads of state gathered in Sirte on 9 September 1999. But he received scant support (nothing at all from South Africa's Thabo Mbeki, then chairman of the AU) and his idea was even ridiculed by some.

The challenge, therefore, to both South Africa and the EU, is to use their leadership roles more effectively to ensure that regional integration in Africa is transformed from being a totem of African unity to being an authentic instrument of progress, development and peace. The political dialogue provided for in the TDCA offer the opportunity for both parties to engage one another on the deficiencies of regional integration in Africa, although it would admittedly take some courage from the EU to raise this issue and pursue it more vigorously. South Africa is the driving force behind the APRM, which is supposed to act as Africa's own watchdog against malpractices. But this mechanism has also proven to be totally ineffective in rogue countries like Zimbabwe, Côte d'Ivoire, the Democratic Republic of the Congo, Sudan and others that have simply resisted external interference aimed at democratic change.

From the above analysis it is therefore clear that the level and depth of integration of the EU outstrip that of the AU by a very wide margin. Apart from some superficial structural similarities, these two organisations differ in most respects and it is doubtful that the world will ever see the EU model of integration replicated in Africa. Unique conditions prevailing in Africa and Europe respectively render this an almost impossible goal. Authentic regional integration in Africa seems possible, but only if based on an architecture still to be formulated. What seems more feasible at this stage is successful integration on a smaller scale, involving sub-continental regions with a high degree of cultural, political, social and economic compatibility, cohesiveness and interdependence, coupled with the necessary political will. Smaller sub-regional experiments like ECOWAS, COMESA and the SADC should find it easier than their big brother to overcome the structural handicaps as well as the political and economic ailments. The much smaller and compact SACU is so far perhaps the most successful attempt at regional integration in Africa, confirming and emphasizing the need for a step-by-step approach that will create spill over effects into the rest of Africa.

Pluralism and diversity in terms of culture, language, religion, etc. are certainly part of the African integration problem, but not the whole problem. It is to be noted that similar divisions did not stop Europe from making significant progress. Europe's multiple nationalities and cultural identities – the capitalist west, the socialist east, the industrial centre, the Mediterranean south and the Nordic north – though very formidable, were not powerful enough to stop the progression towards ever greater unity. But this was a long and drawn-out process, above all made possible by historical experiences, moral and intellectual compatibility, high levels of economic and technological growth, modernization and competitiveness, multilateralism and, most importantly, the overarching quest for Immanuel Kant's "eternal peace". Moreover, what made integration easier in Europe than in Africa was the subordination of nationalism and statehood to the imperatives of universal moral norms pertaining to human rights, good governance and the rule of law. Africa is not yet ready to accept this new paradigm. Therefore, for as long as African states give precedence to the traditional Westphalian system of statehood and sovereignty over the imperatives of universal morality and good governance, mostly at the behest of uncertain and power hungry leadership, authentic integration on this great continent will remain a political myth. This is why the OAU, in spite of its pan-Africanist genesis, failed its mission. The formation of the new AU was an effort to address the shortcomings of its predecessor. Its limited peacekeeping exercises in Burundi and Darfur do point to a new approach to regional cooperation, but while so many other problems remain unresolved, it is premature to expect an integration triumph. The AU certainly has much to learn from the EU concerning successful regionalism. However, it should not seek to duplicate the EU in Africa, but rather to use it as a benchmark of what could be achieved if guided by the political will to succeed.

In Africa, as in Europe, the key variables of success will also be peace, democracy, good governance, modernization, economic progress and, most importantly, the participation of civil society. In conjunction with NEPAD and the various sub-regional organisations, the AU ought to be leading Africa towards these goals. But recent confusing and conflicting statements by African leaders on the much-vaunted APRM to oversee good governance, respect for human rights and good economic management, indicate that they are not yet ready to accept the full consequences of regional integration. What is often described in Africa as regional integration is more particularly regional cooperation. But as the European experience has shown, success comes gradually and alternating failures and successes should be expected in the way forward. In the EU, exemplary leadership and vision has always made the difference at times of a crisis or challenge. As particularly demonstrated by Jean Monnet, Robert Schuman, Paul Henri Spaak and Jacques Delors, regional integration and community formation require champions of supranationalism to challenge narrow nationalist instincts of reactionary leaders. In Africa, the culture of supranationalism does not yet exist.

Africa can hardly endure another false start by the AU and NEPAD. As already indicated, the EU model is not ready-made for Africa. African leaders who believe that Africa should copy the EU should perhaps look not so much at the EU's grand structure, but rather at the way in which its member states have succeeded in finding a practical way to reconcile and blend national sovereignty, intergovernmentalism and supranationalism.

A major problem facing African politics is how to deal with rising expectations among the African masses and new elites. Bureaucrats and politicians presently exclusively drive regional integration in Africa, with civil society out in the cold. The Pan-African Parliament, which supposedly must deal with the latter issue, is neither democratic nor representative. Given the groundwork laid by pan-Africanism and the notion of African unity, a more people-centred regional integration process would seem to be within reach. But this stumbles over a strong residue of authoritarianism in many African states. In the EU, strengthening a common European identity and establishing a participatory democracy enjoy high priority. Addressing the European Parliament on 14 September 1999, Romano Prodi, president of the European Commission, said: "What we now need is to build a union of hearts and minds, underpinned by a strong shared sentiment of a common destiny". Whether the introduction of the PAP will help to narrow the gap, remains to be seen. When looking at the experience of the EU parliament, the chances seem very slim. Perhaps Africa should focus on doing things on a more modest, but practical and workable scale, as was the case with the ECSC, which served as the thin end of the wedge to break the stranglehold of vested interests, statecentrism and narrowly defined sovereignty.

Chapter 8
The European Union and NEPAD: From failed promises to partnership

Introduction

Since Thabo Mbeki took over the South African presidency in 1999 from his illustrious predecessor, Nelson Mandela, African and Third World causes have been his major political pursuit. In contrast to the founding fathers of pan-Africanism who pursued the Kwame Nkrumah dictum "seek ye first the political kingdom", Mbeki casts himself as a neo-pan-Africanist seeking the economic kingdom for the ailing continent. He articulates the idea of building a new, progressive and modernised Africa, an Africa relieved from poverty, backwardness and political decay, and swimming in the main current of world politics and economics. Mbeki defines his primary goals mainly in terms of the aspirations of the developing countries, with issues such as poverty, debt relief, racism and underdevelopment high on his political agenda. All the main strands of his foreign policy join together in his grand vision for Africa. He introduced and popularised the idealistic notion of an African Renaissance; he is the seminal thinker behind and the principal author of NEPAD; the foremost African peacemaker; the founding father and first chairman of the AU; a main player in the NAM, Africa's strongest voice in the debate between the rich North and poor South; and the *über-diplomat* who has succeeded in placing Africa high on the global agenda.

Getting support for NEPAD from the developed nations is, therefore, an important aspect of Mbeki's diplomatic agenda. So far, his success has been remarkable as both the G8 and the EU embraced the NEPAD concept with enthusiasm, although the substantive support in terms of development aid required for making it work is still lacking.

The European Union's policy towards NEPAD

The historical deficiencies of its own development policies are apparently being recognized by the EU, hence its enthusiastic support of NEPAD. It sees South Africa as an important link, mechanism and catalyst in its effort to improve the lot of the developing nations. As stated by Commissioner Peter Mandelson, South Africa is the pivot between the world's more advanced and more vulnerable developing countries.[1]

Although NEPAD operates on a continental scale (it has been adopted by the AU), regional organisations are earmarked to play an important role in the promotion of its goals. NEPAD is of considerable importance in the context of European Union/South African relations. For the EU, NEPAD is significant mainly because it corresponds with and reinforces its own development mission and philosophy; South Africa, as the leading African country, is the main driving force behind the initiative.

The South African president, Thabo Mbeki, stepped onto the African scene with his vision of an African Renaissance and launched NEPAD in conjunction with Nigeria's Olusegun Obasanjo, Senegal's Abdoulaye Wade, Algeria's Abdelaziz Bouteflika and Egypt's Hosni Mubarak. NEPAD goes further than previous multilateral African rescue plans insofar as it speaks of good governance, accountability, economic growth, democracy, human rights, peace and security; of partnership rather than dependence and subservience. It is not hostile to controversial Structural Adjustment Programmes, WTO rules, or globalisation. NEPAD can also boast African ownership and an African pedigree, which cannot be said about previous rescue plans. It is indeed out of Africa and for Africa.[2]

This new approach was welcomed by the world, particularly the EU and the G8. The EU embraced NEPAD because it agreed with many of its own ideals and the policies it has pursued since the early days of the Yaoundé Agreement in the 1970s. Poverty reduction is the central theme underlying these policies. According to an EU publication: "The EU will use its money where there is the greatest chance of alleviating poverty; it will concentrate grant money on the poorest countries and on the poorest parts of the population."[3]

This policy is shared by multilateral entities, including the IMF, the World Bank, the United Nations' development programme, the G8 and individual EU member states. The EU rec-

---

1 *Pretoria News: Business Report*, 13 February 2006, p. 17
2 See Olivier, "Is Thabo Mbeki Africa's saviour?", p. 815–828.
3 European Commission, "Southern Africa and the European Union", Series DE 78, p. 4.

BOX 17   NEPAD: THE BASICS

Preconditions for development:
- Peace, security, democracy, and good governance (Peer Review)
- Economic and corporate governance (Peer Review)
- Regional cooperation and integration

Priority sectors:
- Infrastructure
- Information and communications technology
- Human development and poverty reduction
- Health and education
- Agriculture
- Diversification of exports
- Market access in industrialised countries

Mobilising resources:
- Increasing domestic private savings
- Improved management of public finances to raise public savings
- Enhancing inflows of external resources through expanded debt relief and increased official aid flows, as well as private flows

The NEPAD steering committee:
- Southern Africa: Botswana, South Africa, Mozambique
- North Africa: Egypt, Algeria, Tunisia
- West Africa: Senegal, Mali, Nigeria
- East Africa: Mauritius, Rwanda, Ethiopia
- Central Africa: Gabon, Cameroon, Republic of Congo
- The African Union

ognizes that the main flaw in previous development plans, Lomé in particular, was the lack of African ownership: what had been agreed in Brussels also had to be put into effect in Africa and with African acquiescence. Failure was, therefore, almost a foregone conclusion. As is pointed out by the EU ambassador in South Africa, Michael Lake, "[t]here must be a connecting rod between the wheel and the engine. NEPAD can now become the missing link in the EU development policies".[4]

---

4 M. Lake, "Putting the partnership into Nepad", seminar paper (SA/EU Study Association, Pretoria, 22–23 May 2003), p. 5.

Since NEPAD's inception, the EU has been in dialogue with its African partners to translate NEPAD's vision into concrete actions, with the overarching aim to reach the UN target of halving, by 2015, the number of people living in extreme poverty and suffering from hunger. In view of the fact that the EU provides 55% of ODA and more than two-thirds of grant aid, and that it is the world's largest donor of humanitarian aid, this has become a very important partnership.

The EU's interest has been raised particularly by NEPAD's high degree of African ownership. Ownership by Africa has given the signal to the EU that development strategies would be suitable to local conditions and that their impact would be sustainable over time. The lack of participation of recipient countries in the design of development assistance programmes has in the past often led to reduced efficiency of resource utilisation and limited effectiveness of development initiatives. Donor countries blamed recipient states for bad governance and administrative inefficiencies, only to in return hear complaints about inadequate funding, lack of coordination, duplication of effort and absence of participatory arrangements. Indeed, there is growing consensus that the failure of previous "African rescue plans" hatched off-shore to Africa can be attributed to a combination of the following factors:
- Lack of ownership in the design and implementation of programmes
- Ineffective management of financial resources
- Limited accountability and effectiveness in implementation
- Inadequate monitoring and evaluation.

For much the same reasons, the EU's Lomé Agreements with the ACP states, which started as far back as 1975, failed in important aspects to produce the desired results; hence the introduction of a new dispensation under the Cotonou Agreement in 2000. The goals and priorities of Cotonou correspond with those of NEPAD. Both prioritise poverty reduction, conflict prevention, good governance and enhancing governing capacity. From the operational side then, both NEPAD and the Cotonou action plan emphasize:
- Promotion of democracy and good political governance
- Strengthening of economic and corporate governance
- Development of agriculture and market access
- Human resource development (primarily through health and education)
- Investment in infrastructure
- Environmental protection
- Securing adequate resource flows.

The EU is closely connected with G8 initiatives and the practical follow-up of the Kananaskis Action Plan is already advancing with promising results. The EU is presently looking at methods whereby its partnership with NEPAD can be bolstered and institutionalised, including, in particular, contractual arrangements to implement specific regional and national initiatives. The EU does not intend to set up new agreements or instruments because it believes that these are already in place and only need to be better exploited.

NEPAD has identified increased market access as a key prerequisite for African development. Investment, growth and full integration of Africa in the world economy must be promoted. The EU market is already by far the most open market for African exports. Duty and quota free access for many African exports to Europe has been a reality for numerous years. The EU realizes, however, that more needs to be done to fast-track Africa's integration in the global economy and that Africa should get a better deal from the ongoing negotiations within the WTO framework. The EU will help to equip Africa with the necessary policy and implementation tools that will allow it to profit more from the opportunities offered by global trade liberalization.

One specific area in which the EU can play an important role is capacity building. Returning from the G8's 2003 Evian meeting, President Thabo Mbeki welcomed the billions of dollars and euros pumped into Africa but raised questions about the capacity of the continent to spend the money. "This process has put a big burden on Africa to produce results. I think we have bitten off more than we can chew".[5] In direct response, the European Commission has agreed to start a global fund of €2 million for capacity building in African states. The EU also reacted constructively to NEPAD's identification of peace and security as a precondition for African development and has recently approved a grant of €10 million as an initial contribution to the AU's Peace and Security Agenda.

Warning lights

The EU is committed to contribute towards the success of NEPAD. The forging of an effective African-EU partnership is a strategy that is consistent with the more recent European tradition of participatory development. Within Europe, the promotion of "convergence and social cohesion" is backed-up with so-called "Com-

---

5 Quoted in *Business Day*, 2 June 2003, p. 1.

munity support frameworks". These practices serve to assist the less developed regions of the Community as well as the pre-accession countries of Eastern Europe, and these tested principles are now being extended to Cotonou and NEPAD. The potential for convergence is clearly there, although taking into account past disappointments and failures, the EU should keep its powder dry before prematurely saluting the arrival of a new era.

Ideology seems to be a stumbling block in the way of open-ended cooperation and notions of Eurocentrism and Africanism still cloud the scene. The ghosts of colonialism, neo-colonialism and the "Washington consensus" still loom large in the background. This is something that NEPAD is trying to overcome through the idea of "partnership" in the pursuit of development, security and welfare. The EU and the G8 are presently the most active supporters of NEPAD. Much of this support is conditioned upon Africa's own acceptance of norms and codes of state behaviour (such as good governance, democratic standards, respect for the rule of law and human rights, and sound economic and public administration) that are essentially universal. If Africa abides by these principles, they will certainly help to strengthen the partnership. Unfortunately, aberrations under the Mugabe regime in Zimbabwe are problematic. The EU's monitoring team during the Zimbabwean presidential elections concurred with other observers that the election results were rigged and that Robert Mugabe stole the election. However, these findings were pooh-poohed by Mugabe and because the EU could not come up with a strategy to apply meaningful pressure, they were not of much consequence.

Another dark cloud is the faltering application of NEPAD's (now under the auspices of the AU) APRM. The APRM will, in theory, allow AU member states to place pressure on members of NEPAD to adhere to the normative criteria of the plan. The idea behind peer review is similar to that of the EU's Growth and Stability Pact, which can "name, shame, and ultimately put pressure on countries to adhere to issues of economic and political governance".[6] AU membership will not put states under an obligation to sign the NEPAD declaration on peer review. Participation will be strictly voluntary. This mechanism initially caused great optimism in EU and G8 circles, but this was soon dampened when Mbeki declared that the APRM would no longer fulfil a political function. Governments will have to make their own requests to be reviewed. As the APRM will be voluntary, it will obviously not be applied in serious cases where it is most neces-

---

6 J. Katzenellenbogen, "Nepad: The revolution in accountability", *Business Day*, 10 June 2002, p. 9.

sary, like Zimbabwe, the Democratic Republic of the Congo, Sierra Leone, Liberia, Libya, Burundi, Rwanda, Sudan, etc. Namibian Prime Minister Theo-Ben Guribab speaks about "the manifestly deceptive issue of NEPAD's so-called Peer Review Mechanism", which he says must be consigned "to the dustbin of history as a sham". He continues: "I see it as a misleading, new name for an old, discredited structural adjustment fiasco".[7] A minority of African countries, mostly the more stable and democratic ones, have signed on to the APRM. It is hoped that if they are rewarded for good behaviour, others may also end the aberrations of the past.

Many plans, few solutions

The diagnosis of Africa's many ills was made long ago and has been repeated many times over the years. There has also been a plethora of prescriptions as to how to deal with these ills. Outstanding among these diagnoses and prescriptions were:
- The meeting of the African heads of state in Monrovia in July 1979, which led to the Lagos Plan of Action and the Final Act of Lagos for the economic development of Africa in July 1980
- The World Bank's so-called Berg Report of 1981: "Accelerated Development in Sub-Saharan Africa: An agenda for Action"
- The Economic Commission for Africa's (ECA) Priority Programme for Economic Recovery 1986–1990, converted later into the United Nations Program of Action for Africa's Economic Recovery and Development, and followed up in 1989 by the ECA's The African Alternative Framework to Structural Adjustment Program for Socio-Economic Recovery and Transformation
- The 1989 Arusha conference on Popular Participation for Democracy in Africa, which led to the production of the African Charter for Popular Participation for Development
- The 1989 World Bank Report on Sub-Saharan Africa: "From Crisis to Sustainable Growth – A long-term perspective study"
- The 1991 United Nations New Agenda for Development in Africa in the 1990s
- The 2001 New Partnership for Africa's Development (NEPAD), initiated by Algeria, Egypt, Nigeria, Senegal and South Africa.

---

7   Quoted by Lake, p. 8.

Over and above these studies and reports, there have been the optimistic declarations of the UN General Assembly of a UN Development Decade for the 1960s, followed by a second Development Decade for 1970–1980. These Development Decades envisaged minimum aggregate national income growth rates of 5% and 6% respectively. In this context one should also mention the UN Emergency Recovery and Growth Programmes of the 1980s; the World Bank's African Special Programmes of 1980–1990; and the Highly Indebted Poor Country Programmes covering most of sub-Saharan Africa.

Although all the abovementioned rescue plans and ODA programmes had their own peculiar nuances and motivations, with the exception of the good governance and democracy aspects, they shared a broad common theme that echoed the basic prescriptions of the 1979 Lagos Plan, namely to

- Promote economic and social integration of African economies to enhance self-reliance and self-centred development
- Create national, sub-regional and regional institutions in pursuit of self-reliance
- Give primacy to human resources development
- Place science and technology at the centre of Africa's developmental processes
- Ensure self-reliance in food production, and guarantee the African people proper and adequate nutrition, together with other basic needs for a civilised standard of living
- Undertake proper planning in all sectors of development – particularly agriculture, industry, and the environmentally sound use of natural resources – with the aim of achieving modern economies at national, sub-regional and regional levels.

In tandem with these development plans and strategies, multilateral and bilateral aid programmes, referred to by some writers as the Development Merchant System (DMS), proliferated. These broadly followed the dictates of the national self-interests of the donor country or the specific foreign policy and security requirements of the multilateral organisations. Outstanding among the ODA programmes were those of the European Community and its member states. These programmes had an early origin, but were accelerated in the mid-1970s and legally defined and formalised by the Maastricht Treaty. In general, the EC's development policy reflected a mixture of altruism, benevolence and self-interest. It aimed to

- Redress the inequities and injustices of the colonial period

- Help ACP countries to enter the mainstream of world economics
- Stimulate development in the ACP countries
- Spread European economic influence to the developing world.

Continued marginalization of Africa from the globalisation process and the poverty of the vast majority of its peoples constitute a serious threat to global stability. The consequences of not taking action are high, not only for Africa, but also for Europe. Indeed, the Pisani Memorandum of October 1982 defined the EC objectives under the general heading "peace throughout the world".[8]

The EC development programme found strong expression in the Yaoundé Conventions (1963–1974), and more profoundly in the four Lomé Conventions (1975–2000). However, Lomé did not live up to expectations. Cotonou introduced various innovations to Lomé. Most important among them were the emphasis on partnership, ownership, poverty reduction and a clear association between the political dimension, trade and development.

A notable later addition to the prescriptions of the Lagos Plan was the aspect of good governance. African governments were generally reluctant to buy fully into Structural Adjustment Programmes (SAPs) initially strongly emphasised by the World Bank's Berg Report.[9] It was only after the fall of the Berlin Wall in 1989 that the Lagos Plan's silence about good governance was broken. The Arusha conference on Popular Participation for Democracy in Africa and the subsequent African Charter for Popular Participation and Development conceded that democracy was the *sine qua non* for the continent's development and its economic recovery. Since then the resistance, misgivings and alarm on the part of many African governments and scholars against the introduction of SAPs receded. A compromise was sought in the Economic Commission for Africa's Priority Programme for Economic Recovery 1986–1990, which was later converted into the United Nations Program of Action for Africa's Economic Recovery and Development. These programmes acknowledged that democracy was indeed a cardinal issue in Africa's development. The Cairo Declaration, following the Africa-Europe Summit of April 2000, states (Article 42): "We affirm that democratisation, development and the protection of fundamental freedoms and human rights are inter-related and mutually reinforcing".

---

8 Weidenfeld & Wessels, p. 68.
9 World Bank, "Accelerated development in sub-Saharan Africa – An agenda for action" (Washington D.C., 1981).

Both NEPAD and Cotonou also see as a necessary condition for sustained development the existence of an environment that is politically stable and respectful of human rights, democratic principles, the rule of law and good governance. The fact, however, that NEPAD's Peer Review Mechanism is still being resisted by 30 African states is an indication that the acceptance of democracy, human rights and good governance as crucial for Africa's revival, is not yet a foregone conclusion.

Even so, when looking across the spectrum of these plans and proposals for African development, there is a notable albeit not total consensus on *what* should be done, but great disagreement on *how* it should be done. Central to the "how" question has been the denial of Africans' fundamental right to make decisions about their own future. But, as Adebayo Adedeji observes: "This denial would have been ameliorated if the African leaders had shown the commitment to carry out their own development agenda. But given their excessive external dependence, their narrow political base, and their perennial failure to put their money where their mouth is, the implementation of these plans has suffered from benign neglect. Lacking the resources and the will to soldier on self-reliantly, they abandoned their own strategies".[10] Kenya's Anyang' Nyong'o remarks: "Any attempts to come to terms with this unequal and structurally 'under developing' relationship called for drastically new arrangements in international relations in which Africa needed to recapture her role as a subject and not an object of her own history".[11]

During the last decade or so, the necessity for "new arrangements" has been precipitated by, among others, the following:
- The end of the Cold War in 1989
- South Africa's democratisation since 1994
- Thabo Mbeki's call for an African Renaissance
- Intensification of globalisation and interdependence
- The developing world's resistance against unequal globalisation, "neo-liberalism" and the so-called "Washington consensus"
- African realisation that colonialism can no longer be blamed for African decay
- Afro-pessimism and African marginalization.

---

10 A. Adedeji, "From the Lagos Plan of Action to the New Partnership for Africa's Development, and from the Final Act of Lagos to the Constitutive Act: Whither Africa?", paper given at conference of African Scholars Forum for Envisioning Africa (Nairobi, 2000), quoted in P. Anyang' Nyong'o, "From the Lagos Plan of Action to Nepad: The dilemmas of progress in independent Africa", conference paper, Renaissance South Africa Outreach Programme Continental Experts Meeting, Pretoria, 17–19 June 2002, p. 4.
11 Anyang' Nyong'o, p. 4.

So, as the 20th century drew to a close, African leadership showed a new readiness to commit themselves to Africa's own development agenda; NEPAD at once became the flagship of this new allegiance.

Partnership: A new way or a new promise?

At the same time, the European Union came forward with the new post-Lomé ACP/EU Partnership Agreement signed in Cotonou in June 2000. These developments reflect a remarkable convergence between African and EU thinking about a new way forward. A better understanding between Africa and Europe emerged, an understanding that is particularly epitomised by the Cairo Declaration and the Cairo Plan of Action of 2000. Indeed, a new momentum and a new *raison d'être* to an EU-Africa dialogue (which hardly matured in the past) were established by the landmark conference in Cairo. These developments also brought greater consensus on the connection between the "what" and the "how" of African development.

The new philosophy was articulated as follows by the European Commission: "The success of the EU-Africa dialogue and the progress achieved should not be measured in terms of its capacity to identify new projects but in its capacity to develop common understanding on key issues and to facilitate the elaboration of proposals and their follow up in the appropriate frameworks".[12]

The new paradigm for the Euro/African development cooperation is essentially based on the concept of partnership. NEPAD seeks to succeed where other programmes failed by its being African owned. The same approach underpins Cotonou. As stated by EC Commissioner Poul Nielsen at the time of the conclusion of the agreement: "Partnership goes hand-in-hand with ownership and mutual confidence .... Each country must own and be accountable for its policies." NEPAD, therefore, fits this role and "is a call to the rest of the world to partner Africa in her own development on the basis of her own agenda and programme of action. It is thus a framework for a new partnership with the rest of the world."[13]

Both the G8 (with four European members) and the EU have welcomed NEPAD as a credible plan for Africa's economic re-

---

12 European Commission, "Building an African-EU partnership for action", unpublished discussion paper, May 2004, p. 4.
13 P. Nielson, "The new agreement will benefit the poorest", *ACP/EU Courier*, Special Issue: Cotonou Agreement (September 2000), p. 3.

newal and good governance. The EU also regards NEPAD as the effective vehicle for pursuing the MDGs as well as the objectives of the Cairo Plan. The Kananaskis G8 summit of July 2002 proposed an elaborate action plan for the promotion of trade, investment, sustainable development and capacity building. In this respect Europe is looked upon to take the lead. Its long-standing tradition of development cooperation, with specific reference to the EU's model for pre-accession countries and assistance programmes for the less developed regions of the Community, qualifies it for this role.

Since NEPAD's inception, the EU has been in dialogue with African partners to translate NEPAD's vision into concrete actions. The convergence between NEPAD and Cotonou constitutes an empowerment formula in the field of African development and is in itself a manifestation of partnership. Both place the emphasis on engagement as the only realistic way forward and believe that partnership, rather than dependence and subservience, must be the mode of these engagements. Furthermore, both prioritise poverty reduction, conflict prevention, good governance, the enhancement of government and the involvement of civil society.

Conclusion

The quest for an African revival is an old but unsuccessful one. There has been alternating periods of optimism and pessimism about Africa's post-colonial future. There has also been a plethora of plans and programmes, many aspirations and many disappointments. Now we have NEPAD and Cotonou and a new development paradigm based on partnership. It is, of course, far too early to tell whether the partnership paradigm is the Holy Grail of Africa's revival. There are already pessimistic forebodings about NEPAD. According to the World Economic Forum: "Businesses and other stakeholders in Africa have tried to cajole NEPAD to be more responsive to the needs of the continent; but with patchy success. There is a sense of disillusionment about NEPAD. It has lost steam, and is seen as an ethos rather than a programme of action. It has no implementation capacity".[14] An important factor that seems to be conveniently ignored in the African development equation is that the continent is too large and diverse for a comprehensive, one-step and all-inclusive revival, with or without partnership with powerful external role

---

14 Quoted in *Sunday Times: Business Times*, Johannesburg, 28 May 2006, p. 4

players. A selective and gradual approach seems to be more appropriate. Deviant cases, the proverbial rotten apple among Africa's 53 states, will always be present. In the past Africa has shown a stronger commitment to unity than to the need to get rid of that rotten apple. The new partnership paradigm will not work unconditionally. It should be applied selectively: good behaviour should be rewarded adequately and the willing partners should be first in line for development assistance. EU experience after centuries of conflict has demonstrated to us that a coalition of the likeminded, observing common enforceable political, economic and moral codes, could prove to be the difference. What Africa needs more than anything else at the moment, is to achieve some success to boost its image. This might happen if the new partnership paradigm concentrates on those countries that have the will, the leadership and the potential to succeed. If the principle of the lowest common denominator remains the highest law, the partnership formula will probably go the same way as other rescue plans in the past 50 years.

Chapter 9
An assessment of European Union policy towards South Africa

Introduction

As a multilateral organisation with a restricted mandate regarding foreign policy making, the European Union's role in South Africa is unique in many respects. This has much to do with the way in which Europe operates in world affairs. EU member states have wide ranging foreign policy powers, while Brussels' jurisdiction is restricted mainly to multilateral issues, external trade, economics, development, monitoring and campaigning against weapons of mass destruction, and supporting regional peace-keeping and peace-making efforts. At the same time, member states are free to follow their own development aid programmes (ODA), as many of them do, duplicating rather than reinforcing the EU's work.[1] While the EU's foreign policy represents the sum total of its members, the reverse is not true as members more often than not pursue their own interests and agendas. In the end, this diffuse way of foreign policy making in Europe has a debilitating effect on both the EU and its members, with the result that its role in world affairs is far smaller than it should be. It does not take any flight of the imagination to realize that if Europe were to pool its foreign policy resources and act in concert as a "United States of Europe", it could find itself in the higher echelon in the hierarchy of global politics. In a way, therefore, the EU presently plays the role of a gentle giant in a world dominated by the vicissitudes of *realpolitik*. In spite of its

---

1 M. Olivier "Development cooperation agreements between the EU, its member states and SA: An assessment of the legal requirements", unpublished paper delivered at ECSASA Conference, University of the Western Cape, 12 February 2002, pp. 1–2.

major role as an aid donor and trading partner in Africa, it plays second fiddle to the G8, America, Britain and France regarding the debate and setting of the political agenda for policies about international involvement to promote development in Africa. And notwithstanding the fact that its relations with South Africa are amicable and substantial, particularly as far as economic content is concerned, its political-diplomatic influence is less than it should be, or could be expected. In fact, South Africa's interaction on presidential and ministerial level is noticeably more intensive and regular with individual member countries than with the European Commission in Brussels.

Who gets what?

In the context of EU/South African relations, important questions to seek answers for are the following:
- What does the EU get or expect in return for its constructive role in South Africa?
- What does South Africa get or expect to get out of its relations with the EU?
- Does EU involvement in South Africa make a difference to the latter's welfare and security?

When doing an assessment of this kind, it should be stated at the outset that in the amorphous field of foreign policy and diplomacy, it is always extremely difficult to evaluate with some precision what is being achieved. Precision and clarity are hardly possible because of the dominant role the vast range of subjective elements play in the making of foreign policy. Moreover, the complex interplay among the various strands and dimensions of foreign policy and the generally opaque and open-ended nature of diplomatic activity restrict exact analysis. Judgment must predominantly rely on the impressionistic assessment of the many subjective elements affecting decision-making and action. These include ideologically determined national interests, enigmatic behavioural attitudes, unpredictable political mood swings, propagandistic rhetoric, idiosyncratic elements in elite and bureaucratic culture, and rhetorical obfuscation. In the absence, therefore, of a calculus of scientific exactness, assessments of foreign policy results must mainly rely on rough benchmarks and *ex post facto* appraisals.

If this impressionistic estimation is generally positive, as in the case of the present state of EU/South African relations, policy makers and diplomats on both sides would not be unduly concerned, even if they did realize that there was room for improvement. They are generally ruled by the diplomatic imperative of maintaining a public image of a good, mutually beneficial and dependable relationship. If there are shortcomings, these can be worked on as part of the ongoing diplomatic process, mostly away from the public eye. For the analyst it is important, however, to discern discrepancies, if there are any, between the operational and the normative or possible. In the case of EU/South African relations, probably as with all other configurations of bilateral international relationships, the prevailing situation is not the best it could be. But while an ideal situation is not possible, it is certainly feasible to address the obvious aspects where improvements could be made, given the existence of the necessary political will.

An important, yet asymmetrical relationship

South African relations with Europe reflect a dual character: multilateral EU/South African relations focusing mainly on economic, trade, development and humanitarian aspects, and bilateral relations with each of the member states, covering the entire gamut of foreign relations – political, economic and cultural. In spite of the political limitations its treaties impose on EU diplomacy, its relations with South Africa are unique in terms of economic and functional substance, professionalism, consistency and intensity. In these respects, EU/South African relations are in both quality and substance distinguishable not only from conventional bilateral relations, but also from South Africa's relations with other multilateral international bodies like the United Nations, the African Union and specialised agencies.

It is an asymmetrical relationship in the sense that the EU is the much stronger partner, with South Africa the more vulnerable because of its strong dependence on trade and investment with Europe. For example, less than 2% of EU trade is with South Africa, while about 40% of South Africa's trade is with the EU. This makes the EU South Africa's biggest trading partner. In addition, the EU is also the biggest donor of development aid to the country, while European countries are South Africa's biggest direct capital investors. Even so, the EU studiously refrains from exploiting this interdependence asymmetry to enhance its own position in a relationship that has not really developed beyond an amicable, business-like partnership. The EU is arguably entitled to greater "rewards" in the form of a closer friendship, but this has not materialised. It is a situation, therefore, where EU eagerness[2] is not matched by a similar South African response.

The EU is not among South Africa's closest friends and allies. Thus, the South African side of the relationship gives the impression of a distinct attitudinal asymmetry.

However, despite these asymmetries, ongoing relations have been developed that have special advantages to both sides. The EU's involvement in South Africa is more intensive than in any other country in the developing world. It articulates the importance of the relationship as follows: "South Africa's foreign policy is driven by the country's strengthened role on the world stage and its leadership position amongst developing countries in their pursuit of greater equality and equity. On issues such as disarmament, a fairer trading environment, debt relief and racism, South Africa has established itself increasingly as a bridge-builder between the developed and developing world. From an EU perspective, South Africa is considered an increasing close political ally with whom a serious and mutual beneficial dialogue exists, despite differences on certain issues".[3]

To sum up, the following fundamental or strategic considerations guide EU policy:
- Protecting the investment the EU has made over the years into a stable future for South Africa. The EU regards South Africa as "a pole of stability and growth in the Southern African region, which deserves to be supported and strengthened"[4]
- The importance of South Africa's newly found respectability in the world and its general strategic importance as a partner in world politics
- South Africa's leadership role in the Southern African region, Africa in general, and the rest of the developing world, which makes it a valuable ally or partner in international affairs
- In the important but inconclusive North-South debate about the effect of globalisation and poverty relief in the developing world, South Africa's voice carries considerable weight
- South Africa is an excellent testing ground for the EU's development aid and trade policies in emergent markets and the developing world in general
- South Africa is one of the EU's most lucrative trading partners in the developing world.

---

2 See box 18, Towards a European Union-South Africa strategic partnership.
3 Delegation of the European Commission to South Africa, Annual Report (2004), Pretoria, p. 3.
4 European Commission, "Evaluation of the European Commission's Country Strategy for South Africa", p. 1.

BOX 18 TOWARDS A EUROPEAN UNION/SOUTH AFRICA STRATEGIC PARTNERSHIP[5]

> Over the last 12 years, South Africa and the EU "have built a close relationship, based on shared values, mutual respect and interests. The two partners share political and ethical values such as democracy, human rights, respect for the rule of law and good governance, tolerance, equality and a commitment to fight poverty and social exclusion. They agree on the basic economic principles of the social market economy, sustainable development, free trade, and an equitable international economic order. They are both actively committed to an agenda of peace and stability, democratisation, governance and combating poverty throughout the African continent. They both believe in multilateral solutions to international conflicts and have an interest in making sure that the voice of the developing and emerging countries is heard on the international scene. Building on these values and interests the EU and South Africa have developed over the years a multifaceted, fairly comprehensive 'mosaic' partnership, based on the Trade, Development and Cooperation Agreement (TDCA) between South Africa, the European Community and its Member States. The purpose [of policy] is, therefore, to give the EU a comprehensive, coherent and coordinated long-term framework for its relations with the Republic of South Africa, that is mindful of South Africa's traumatic past, of its role as an anchor country in the region and its unique position on the continent and on the global scene, while building on "The European Consensus on Development" and on the "Strategy for Africa".

For South Africa, the value of EU relations lies primarily in the economic field. Before the regime change in 1994, the scope of these relations were restricted and limited, partly because of lack of interest and partly because of the EU's discomfort with South Africa's domestic policies. At the same time, however, some powerful EU member states, particularly the United Kingdom, France, Germany and Italy, maintained strong trade as well as cultural ties with the country and joined the anti-apartheid sanctions campaign rather belatedly. These relations, particularly in the cultural field, were maintained with the minority white South African population of European descent, giving the im-

---

5 Communication from the European Commission to the Council, the European Parliament and the European Economic and Social Committee, unpublished memorandum, Brussels, 30 March 2006.

pression that they were sympathetic towards the apartheid regime and reluctant to give its support to the liberation movement. Under the new post-1994 dispensation this situation was completely reversed: for all practical purposes white South Africans became marginalised, with the EU's attention being totally focussed on accommodating the new government and helping the previously disadvantaged black section of the population by way of its aid policy. However, in spite of the fact that the economic substance of the relations, aid and trade in particular, increased with leaps and bounds with the post-1994 government, the "special relationship" that had previously existed between Europe and South Africa has not again been achieved.

The following main reasons account for the absence of a close or special relationship between the EU and South Africa:
- Ideological predilections on the part of the South African government seem to stand in the way of such a relationship. The historical fact that European nations were the former colonisers, who later developed close economic, political and cultural ties with the white minority government and the European sector of the South African population, precluded the continuation of a similar close relationship with the new ANC government. The ANC's background and belief system prescribed a new and different relationship. The Eurocentrism of the old regime had to make way for the Afrocentrism of the new regime, emphasising the cultural and ideological fault lines that divide Europe and Africa and proclaiming the emergence of an African Renaissance. Eurocentrism thus became a pejorative notion in the political lexicon of ideological purists in the ANC government. This attitude places its ideological interests in Africa and other developing regions in the Southern hemisphere before economic and security interests with Western nations, preventing a close relationship with the latter and imposing some restraint on contemporary EU/South African relations. In terms of this policy and the sentiments that underpin it, countries that contribute almost nothing to South Africa's welfare, and some whose impact is patently negative, for instance Zimbabwe, Cuba and Jean-Bertrand Aristide's Haiti, are emotionally much closer to Pretoria than Brussels. Furthermore, in issues involving the crises in Palestine, Iraq and Iran, South Africa refuses to follow the leadership of American led Western diplomacy.
- The EU joined the sanctions campaign against apartheid South Africa in a fairly late and haphazard way. The ANC,

being in its struggle phase, expected the EU to do more, sooner. Its umbrage showed when Nelson Mandela and other ANC leaders refused to meet Sir Godfrey Howe, then president of the EC Council of Foreign Ministers, when he visited South Africa in 1986. While moralistic altruism was certainly an important rationale behind the EU's assistance to the victims of apartheid from 1985 onwards, self-interest was lurking in the background. It instituted sanctions against South Africa belatedly because of disunity in its own ranks about the wisdom of sanctions. Some countries were keen supporters of sanctions while others were reluctant to sacrifice their trade connections with South Africa. Eventually, political expediency stepped in when the EU realized that it was falling out of step with the broader international campaign against apartheid. To make amends, substantial aid was given to the victims of apartheid, without any expectation of reciprocity on the EU side, and a rigid sanctions regime was introduced against the South African government of the time. However, while aid continued after 1994, a new competitive trade dimension became part of the policy mix and the moral aspect became somewhat diluted.

- The South African government's posture was also influenced by the EU's relentless, even miserly, pursuance of trade advantages during the TDCA negotiations. What came to the fore here was the hard side of the EU's two-track, Jekyll and Hyde policy. After the euphoria and the international acclamation that followed South Africa's peaceful democratic transformation in 1994, Pretoria probably assumed that the EU and other affluent international actors would fall over their feet to facilitate trade and investment on the best possible terms for a country so long blighted by apartheid. But this was not to happen. South Africa's hopes to become a full member of the Lomé Agreement were dashed, and although the EU's counter offer of a TDCA and qualified Lomé membership (Cotonou after 2000) carried distinct advantages, South Africa did not regard it as a magnanimous gesture. Relations were also soured by the fact that the negotiations for the free trade aspects of the TDCA were difficult, protracted and acrimonious and punctuated by moments of sheer pettiness on the part of the EU negotiators.[6] The spirit and outcome of this negotiation process, which South Africa expected to be

---

6 Davies, "The Department of Trade and Industries perspective", p. 40; Smalberger, pp. 47–51; Keet.

a continuation of the goodwill and understanding demonstrated by the EU's early commitment and contribution to heal the wounds left by apartheid, must have poisoned relations at an early stage. The fact that South Africa's diplomatic mission to the Commission in Brussels has been hopelessly small and understaffed[7] for the task at hand and that Mbeki procrastinated until 2004 before making an official visit to the Commission in Brussels, may also indicate diplomatic pique.

The South African government does not seem at all concerned about the negative impact its ideologically driven foreign policy could have on long-term national interests. Too strong an emphasis on ideology comes at a cost, particularly bearing in mind that the EU contribution is qualitatively and quantitatively far superior to that of South Africa's close ideological friends in Africa and elsewhere in the Southern hemisphere. The country should make better use of the opportunity of having a rewarding partnership with the EU at a relatively low cost and without the need or demand of a matching performance.

It is highly improbable that the EU would engage South Africa on the issue of greater symmetry. In any case, the EU is hamstrung by its lack of super power aura and gravitas and South African policy makers do not feel pressurised to do something special to protect the relationship. Their main aim is to maintain a professionally correct and fairly platonic stance, to operate within the existing diplomatic legal framework, to preserve a stable status quo and to reap the advantages of a secure, predictable relationship.[8]

Trade and development assistance as instruments of European Union policy: Substantial, but not adequate

To promote its interests, the EU relies on cooperation on a wide range of aspects in the trade, economic, political development, culture, science and technology fields. Trade and FDI statistics in particular offer a very clear barometer of the way in which relations are developing. Since the conclusion of the TDCA in 2000, the results have been substantial. The EU is now South Africa's

---

7 S. Schepers, "Missing chances in Europe?", *Leadership Magazine* 249, (June 2003), p. 32.
8 See G. Olivier, "Costly allure of pied piper of ideology", *Business Day*, 30 January 2004, p. 9.

biggest trading partner, accounting for approximately 40% of the country's imports and 30% of its exports. In the period from 1994 to 2000, the EU member states accounted for 30% of FDI into South Africa and about 60% of total South African assets held by foreigners. According to the EU delegation in South Africa, "[t]he EU-SA Trade, Development and Cooperation Agreement (TDCA) continued to strengthen this relationship ... consolidating South Africa as one of Europe's preferred trading partners".[9] The EU is also South Africa's single biggest aid benefactor. Development aid, trade and FDI complement one another in the promotion of EU interests in South Africa: trade and FDI are creators of wealth and diplomatic influence, while development aid creates the favourable atmosphere in which trade can flourish and diplomatic objectives can be pursued more easily. Moreover, some aid money finds its way back into the trade cycle by way of goods and services or through the substantial tenders for development projects, which usually favour the donor. In all these respects relations with South Africa clearly hold special advantages for the EU.

The quantitative inputs of EU development assistance in South Africa, i.e. money and programmes, are quite impressive. Community assistance represents around 25% of all ODA to South Africa. Together with the EIB and EU member states' bilateral assistance, the total is approximately 70% of all ODA to the country.[10] Between 1994 and 1999 the total value of EU aid (including the contributions by the EIB) to South Africa amounted to R7 216 775 000. The second largest contribution was that of America, whose contribution over the same period was R2 494 990 000.[11] The EU's annual aid commitment to South Africa amounts to about €124 million (R992 million). Expressed as percentages of the South African GNP (R1 149.89 billion for 2002/3 at current price levels) EU aid comes to about 0.08%, and trade to about 0.7%. As a percentage of the annual South African budget, total ODA commitments for the period 1994–1999 represented 1–2%.[12]

While the EU generally seems satisfied with the achieve-

---

9 Delegation of the European Commission in South Africa, Annual Report (2002), Pretoria p. 4.
10 European Commission, "South Africa-European Community Country Strategy Paper and Multi-annual Indicative Programme for the period 2003–2005" (Pretoria, Directorate-general for Development, 2003), p. 13.
11 European Commission, "Evaluation of the European Commission's Country Strategy for South Africa", p. 7.
12 European Commission, "South Africa-European Community Country Strategy Paper and Multi-annual Indicative Programme for the period 2003–2005" (Pretoria, Directorate-general for Development, 2003), p. 12.

ments of its South African aid programme,[13] country strategy audits point out that there is room for improvement, particularly with regard to implementation strategies impacting on poverty reduction, social services, regional cooperation, integration and policy dialogue.[14] A more thorough evaluation procedure of programmes seems to be called for, particularly on the output side. Excessive bureaucracy and the lack of decision-making flexibility in the approval and implementation of projects, further blunt EU efforts.[15] The dilemma for donors of taxpayers' money to foreign countries is how to strike a balance between the prevention of mismanagement and bureaucratic flexibility, particularly in countries where corruption and mismanagement are fairly common.

The EU looks critically at its performance in the field of development assistance to South Africa and independent audits are carried out regularly. Generally speaking, donors of ODA are wont to present their contributions in an over-optimistic if not inflated way, emphasizing the money side and the philanthropic intentions while the concrete results mostly remain clouded in obscurity. In the short term, these deficiencies are usually overshadowed by the recipients' appreciation of the apparent magnanimity of the donor, but in the longer term, if results are not noticeable, the whole exercise may go sour: hence the African phenomenon of "aid fatigue". In its internal operations, the EU seems to be well aware of this trap, although its publicity programmes generally overemphasize the quantitative volume of inputs.[16] Very little is said about the measurable holistic impact of its programmes on the key issue areas that obstruct South Africa's development and modernization.

Given the magnitude of South Africa's development problems and needs, the development aid it receives is therefore but a drop in the ocean.[17] On the other hand, the quality and target-

---

13 According to the "Evaluation of the European Commission's Country Strategy for South Africa": "the Commission's implementation of the 2000–2002 MIP (Multi-annual Indicative Programme) is proceeding in a satisfactory way", p. 54.
14 Ibid. pp 55–59.
15 L. Fioramonti, "The European Union promoting democracy in South Africa: Strengths and weaknesses", p. 12.
16 The European Commission's appetite for statistics to explain its development aid in South Africa seems insatiable. However, in spite of the avalanche of statistics it is very difficult to construct a holistic picture because of the random way in which these statistics are presented. In the end, it seems as if the main role of this methodology is to emphasise the magnitude and magnanimity of EU ODA.
17 Total donor aid to South Africa represents less than 3% of the total budget.

ed nature of aid, the professional management and application thereof, and the spill over effect on local expertise may make a positive contribution in the longer term. A study commissioned by the South Africa government showed that "ODA contributed significantly to some key sectors by bringing knowledge and international 'best practice' to SA through technical assistance and capacity building".[18]

It should be borne in mind that ODA has never been a resounding success story in Africa. Notions of aid fatigue are frequently expressed and after almost five decades of development aid, donor countries are still groping about for the optimal approach as one grand development plan is exchanged for another.[19] There is also the rather cynical view that ODA has over the years metamorphosed into a phenomenon with its own separate life and rationale. Critics contend that it is sustained at the behest of the vested interests of an elaborate, institutionalised, costly and cumbersome bureaucratic apparatus that often overshadow those of the developing nations; that it is but a sop to poor countries in an effort to assuage mounting Third World criticism about unfair exploitation by industrialized countries; that it serves as a foreign policy exhibit for donor nations in their quest for international moral prestige and respectability; and that development aid methodology and objectives are dominated by a so-called neo-liberal agenda that lies at the root of contemporary unequal globalisation. One critic equated development aid to the Third World to "shovelling smoke".[20]

Extreme views such as these are naturally often suffused with subjective a priori's, oversimplifications and unsubstantiated premises. Even so, it is an undeniable fact that the track record of ODA in the Third World is a patchy one. Mistakes are repeated, problems are not resolved and poverty, disease and economic decay in developing countries continue to take their toll, while contributions by donor countries remain hopelessly inadequate. A fundamental rethink of the development aid paradigm has therefore become an urgent matter. The fact that NEPAD is so eagerly embraced by the EU and G8 countries is a clear indication that they are extremely anxious to link up with a better recipe for African development than what they themselves have so far offered.

---

18 European Commission, "South Africa-European Community Country Strategy Paper and Multi-annual Indicative Programme for the period 2003–2005" (Pretoria, Directorate-general for Development, 2003), p. 12.
19 See G. Olivier, "One plan will not fit all Africa", *Business Day*, 7 February 2005, p. 12.
20 Black, p. 64.

Only time will tell how successful ODA in South Africa or the Southern African region has been. Obviously, given the relatively small and inadequate contributions that come the country's way, they will not have a Marshall Aid effect. What may contribute to the success of development aid in South Africa, is the country's more developed and sophisticated socio-economic and infrastructural environment, compared to that of other ACP countries. These types of factors counted largely in favour of the success of Marshall Aid in Europe, but then the magnitude of Marshall Aid was much greater and the commitment stronger. The fact that South Africa was over a period of 350 years never a receiver of donor aid until the time of the regime change in the 1990s, probes the efficacy of donor aid. Yet, fending for itself, it became Africa's most developed, modernised and prosperous country, amidst its being blighted by apartheid. The country's advancement would undoubtedly have been much better was it not for apartheid and the exclusion of the majority black population from the economic mainstream and national reward system. This policy left a distorted socio-economic legacy of a rich white minority and a poor black majority, a situation that called for rectification after the democratic transformation. Accelerated development and affirmative action for the betterment of the daily lives of the many previously disadvantaged South Africans and to guarantee a stable democracy were, therefore, urgently needed. However, South Africa has not received anything even remotely comparable to Marshall Aid. The development aid, investment, loans and humanitarian assistance that started to flow into the country after 1994, have fallen hopelessly short of the expectations aroused by the lavish promises of leaders of the rich industrialised nations that stood in the first row to bask in the glory of South Africa's peaceful and democratic transformation.

From a humanitarian point of view, EU foreign aid, particularly the assistance given to the victims of apartheid, was undoubtedly a magnanimous gesture. Unfortunately, however, even together with aid from other donors, it affected only a selected minority. In terms of the national requirements, it was hopelessly inadequate and erroneously targeted. The EU's initial humanitarian, free-wheeling assistance programme to the victims of apartheid was soon replaced by a new approach under the umbrella of the TDCA, which changed the emphasis to a more systematic, coordinated and cooperative approach, with partnership with the government and various role players being the new preferred *modus operandi*. The sectoral distribution (weighted) of ODA shows that education, government and democracy, agriculture and rural development, business development, health and housing are presently the main targets of total aid distributions. All these sectors are important determinants and multipliers of sustained national development and modernization as well as essential prerequisites for poverty reduction, stable democracy and good governance. Yet the question of adequacy remains unanswered. The spectre of widening income inequality, slow economic growth, inadequate job creation, rampant criminality, corruption, high unemployment and the HIV/AIDS pandemic hangs darkly over South Africa's future development. These problems can be better taken care of by way of greater societal welfare, more wealth creation and redistribution of wealth, something that ODA on its own is incapable of doing. After ten years under the new dispensation and with ODA flowing into the country for the first time, macro indicators of success (poverty, unemployment and economic growth) have declined into negative territory and the scourge of the HIV/AIDS pandemic has become worse. The Southern African regional economic situation also looks bleaker, although the enduring drought and the chaotic Zimbabwean situation are mostly to blame. Logically, the EU's effort to enhance the South African transformation through capacity building[21] in the fields of education, training and good governance should have a multiplying impact and spill over to other areas to benefit the nation as a whole. However, there are few empirical signs of this happening yet. Perhaps it is too early to judge, but given the relative smallness of the total ODA contribution in the context of the entire economy and in proportion to the national development problem, the real impact on a national scale on particularly GDP growth, poverty relief and unemployment reduction will probably remain small, even negligible.[22] The best scenario seems to be that the involvement of the EU and other aid donors would reinforce and add momentum to the government's own efforts to uplift and develop South Africa's poor and disadvantaged masses in the long-term.[23] In itself, however, ODA offers no panacea.

The EU apparently wants to strengthen the impact of ODA by spreading the reach of its programmes as broadly as possible.

---

21 European Commission, "Country Strategy Paper for South Africa", p. 5.
22 See P. S. Heller, "Making aid work", *Finance and Development*, 42:3 (September 2005), pp. 9–13.
23 Indeed, according to the EC "participation and partnership" "are key to policy implementation". See European Commission, "South Africa-European Community Country Strategy Paper and Multi-annual Indicative Programme for the period 2003–2005" (Pretoria, Directorate-general for Development, 2003), p 11.

The proliferation of programmes under its banner is indeed striking, but at the same time it is not clear what happens on the output side of the aid equation.[24] According to the Community delegation in South Africa's 2002 Annual Report, some 57 separate projects (2000–2006) are being implemented, each with a different theme, at a budgeted cost of €885.5 million. These programmes definitely greatly add to the EU's visibility and prestige in South Africa as a benevolent partner helping the country to move forward. But large chunks of aid that go under the name of "development aid" are essentially humanitarian relief and should, therefore, be judged from a different perspective. These include the EU's programmes for health and population, water and sanitation and parts of its programmes for local economic development and consolidation of democracy, good governance and civil society and regional cooperation. While humanitarian aid and development aid are of course interrelated, the question remains whether the EU's approach is not too diffuse, too thinly spread and too broadly targeted to make the real and lasting impact desired.

A productive but not special relationship

The criteria by which to judge the impact of the EU's role in South Africa are indeed very complex. However, while it is not really a mature relationship, it is a good relationship: rich in substance and serving the interests of both parties well, though clearly more so for South Africa than for the EU. Although the EU has been officially active in South Africa for only a relatively short period, some notable diplomatic successes have been achieved. These include the sound working relationship it has managed to develop with South Africa through the establishment of a formal legal and institutional framework of cooperation, the normalization of diplomatic relations, the launching of the TDCA, South Africa's special membership of the Cotonou Agreement, as well as the conclusion of the Wine and Spirits Agreement and the Scientific Cooperation Agreement.

Although subjective ideological preferences and parameters on South Africa's side put some distance between itself and the EU, a substantial relationship has already been developed since 1994. South Africa does regard it as a close strategic partnership: economic considerations and trade in particular constitute the *raison d'être* of the relationship. With the EU its biggest trading

---

24 See Bratton & Landsberg.

partner by a very wide margin, South Africa seems to argue that the relations are on a sound footing, with the potential for further growth and more material substance. At the same time, the EU responds with positive measures, mainly under the umbrella of the all-encompassing TDCA, backed by unfailing friendly diplomacy. On the surface of things, therefore, there seems to be no immediate problem for either side.

Over the longer term, however, trade and economic considerations alone are not enough to sustain the relationship. The context of EU politics is changing quite rapidly: enlargement, domestic problems in member states, dealing with difficult Eastern neighbours like Russia, and the dangerous unpredictability of events in the Middle East have an increasingly important impact on Brussels' priorities. It is particularly important to bear in mind that while the European Commission is strongly committed to build a strategic partnership with South Africa, other institutions of the EU may not always share the same view. South Africa's distant attitude and ideological predilections are not necessarily helpful in this respect. New realities may in future change the present texture of the relationship. Some of these new realities are already looming in the form of the high cost of enlargement of the EU to include the poorer countries of Central and Eastern Europe;[25] the impact of the slow-down of economic growth and rising unemployment in the EU zone; structural changes in EU economic and fiscal policies and changes in decision-making procedures affecting ODA; new priorities and criteria in the distribution of development aid to countries poorer than South Africa; and the growing uneasiness about African countries' refusal to adopt more acceptable universal standards on democracy, the rule of law and human rights. Accessibility to Fortress Europe's shrinking resource pool from which South Africa and other ACP countries have so richly benefited, may change. South Africa is not at all a key priority in the all-important EU regional strategic equation and may shift to the periphery of the political radar screen if or when the saliency of the latter's immediate regional interests become more pressing.

The prudent and sensible way to go is for South Africa to work continuously and consciously towards a greater measure of reciprocity and balance in the relationship. Broadening and deepening the relationship is clearly in its national interests. And in view of the EU's present receptiveness, such a posture, leading to a more special relationship or perhaps a strategic partner-

---

25 See C. van der Westhuyzen, "Africa and the changing face of the EU: Economic opportunity or threat?", *Global Insight 39*, (October 2004), pp. 1–9.

ship, will bring substantial benefits to the people of South Africa and the security of the state. Bearing in mind that the EU contribution to South Africa's welfare and economic security is far superior to that of the latter's close ideological friends in Africa and elsewhere in the Southern hemisphere, it stands to reason that subjective considerations should yoke a closer relationship. Problems of transformation, rampant poverty, mass unemployment and a menacing HIV/AIDS pandemic cannot be addressed effectively without the necessary economic capacity. The EU plays a key role in this respect and relations with the latter should, therefore, be at the apex of South Africa's foreign policy equation.

For the present, the European Commission argues that the importance of economic, strategic and symbolic advantages of its South African relations outweigh the negatives of the latter's ideological predilections. The diplomatic and material investments it has made in South Africa over the last two decades underline its strong and vested interests in South Africa's stable future, a future that may not yet be fully assured, particularly in the light of the reasons mentioned above and the recent schisms in the ruling ANC/SACP/Cosatu alliance. A foreign policy based on economic diplomacy and engaging the developed world more fully, is therefore of vital importance to South Africa's national security and future stability. Presently, South Africa does actively engage in economic diplomacy, but in a way subsidiary to its ideological pursuits, particularly those in Africa. Its policy towards the EU clearly reflects this debilitating dichotomy. For policy makers, the possible longer-term negative impact of this posture on EU/South African relations may not be apparent or salient at the moment. It is a relationship not yet mature or fully exploited; above all, it is a relationship that should not always be taken for granted. South Africa should invest more in it, especially the private sector, which has because of lack of knowledge and application not yet succeeded in exploiting the European market to its own best advantage[26]. More application and commitment are therefore necessary on the South African side.

Postscript

After the completion of this manuscript, the European Commission issued a proposal concerning the possible creation of a South African/EU Strategic Alliance. This proposal and the South African response to it corroborate the author's analysis that although the relationship between South Africa and the EU has been mutually beneficial, it has lacked the quality of a special relationship and there has been room for improvement, particularly on the diplomatic/political level.

This proposal was preceded by a consensus in the Joint Cooperation Council (an instrument of the TDCA) among South Africa, the European Commission and member states that recent changes in EU/South Africa relations called for a more coherent strategic framework. They adopted "Joint Conclusions" at the 23 November 2004 meeting and a "Joint Report" in November 2005, and agreed that "new steps need to be taken to ensure that South Africa-EU relations develop into a truly strategic partnership that ... would do justice to the role of South Africa as an anchor on the continent and a key player on the international scene".[1]

In the "Communication from the Commission to the Council and the European Parliament" of 28 June 2006, the Commission argued that the goals contained in the TDCA should be augmented by adding a stronger diplomatic/political dimension to the relationship. To this end, it proposed the creation of a multifaceted, comprehensive "EU/South African Strategic Partnership", to come about as a result of "a dynamic development" over time.

The Commission motivated its proposal by stating that "South Africa and the EU share political, social and ethical values such as democracy, human rights, respect of the rule of law and good governance, tolerance, equality, a commitment to fight poverty and social exclusion and the promotion of sustainable development. They agree on the basic economic principles of the social market economy, free trade and an equitable international economic order. They are both actively committed to an agenda of peace and stability, governance, democratisation and combating poverty throughout the African continent. They both believe in multilateral solutions to international conflicts and have an inter-

---

[1] Commission of the European Communities, Communication from the Commission to the Council and the European Parliament: "Towards an EU-South African Strategic Partnership", Brussels, 28 June 2006, p. 6.

est in making sure that the voices of developing and emerging countries are heard on the international scene."[2]

The proposal went on to stress South Africa's important role in the Southern African region, the African continent, and in global politics and added: "South Africa and the EU share much common ground as bridge-builders between North and South, between West and East, between civilisations, peoples and religions. Europe believes it can perform this function better in a partnership with South Africa."[3]

According to the proposal, "the most important element of the proposed Strategic Partnership consists in moving from mere political dialogue to active political cooperation. The South Africa-EU Partnership must become a meeting place for building bridges between two consensus-seeking representatives of the North and the South. Its main purpose must be to enable the two parties to actively seek common ground on issues of mutual interest, support each other's political agendas and take joint political action at regional, African or global level... Today ... relations between South Africa and the EU require more coherence, clear objectives, and a shared forward-looking political vision with a view to strengthening joint political action. The partnership seeks to clearly spell out what both sides can expect from one another on the domestic, regional, continental and global fronts and to do justice to South Africa's and the EU's unique positions in the new globalised world."[4]

A strong underlying theme of the statement is that the partnership would serve the foreign policy interests of both parties, on the domestic, regional, continental and global fronts better than the existing dispensation. The Commission thinks highly of South Africa's "unique" standing in the Southern African region, the African continent, the rest of the developing world and on a global level, and a strategic partnership would, therefore, add leverage and prestige to both parties' foreign policy endeavours.

The proposed strategic partnership seeks to implement this process by
- Bringing the member states, the Community and South Africa together in a single and coherent framework, with clearly and jointly defined objectives, covering all areas of cooperation and associating all stakeholders
- Moving from political dialogue to strategic political cooperation and shared objectives on regional, African and global issues

---
2   Ibid. p. 4.
3   Ibid. p. 10.
4   Ibid. p. 2.

- Enhancing existing cooperation, developing stronger and sustainable economic cooperation, fully implementing the TDCA provisions on trade-related areas and extending cooperation to the social, cultural and environmental fields.

In addition, the Strategic Partnership must build on the MDG Package, The European Consensus on Development and the EU Strategy for Africa by putting at the heart of the political dialogue the progress towards attaining the MDGs, along with governance issues and peace and security at both domestic and international levels.[5]

Depending on discussions with the Council, the European Parliament and the European Economic and Social Committee, the Commission would draw up a draft Action Plan for implementing the strategic partnership, to be submitted to the Joint EU/South Africa Cooperation Council.

In response to the Commission's proposal, the South African government issued a statement on 29 June 2006, declaring that it "welcomes this move as a positive step forward in the process of elevating SA-EU relations. SA and the EU have, since mid 2005, been informally engaging each other on the possibility of elevating their relationship. SA and the EU share many common objectives and positions, and both SA and the EU believe that intensified cooperation will be of mutual benefit... A 'strategic partnership' relationship will allow SA and the EU to engage in more intensive dialogue on political, economic and developmental issues. According to the EC, a strategic partnership with the EU would give SA far greater recognition in Europe's strategic global awareness, as well as in time allow SA to be placed on a high-priority diplomatic footing with the EU. SA-EU relations would thus hold similar importance to those held by the EU and the USA, Canada, China, Russia, India, and Brazil, all of whom have special agreements with the EU. The South African Government anticipates that formal discussions regarding an elevation of relations could commence once the EC has tabled their proposed strategic partnership before the European Council (the Member States), which is expected to happen in late September this year. At such a juncture, SA is committed to being mindful of honoring its multilateral commitments and to consulting with its regional partners on all relevant matters. SA and the EU enjoy a good and mutually beneficial relationship. South Africa is committed to working with the European Union to enhance the rela-

---

5   Ibid. p. 6.

tionship and to work towards stronger cooperation for the achievement of peace, stability and development of the African continent."[6]

The Commission seems to argue that a strategic relationship with South Africa, the strongest, most stable democracy in Africa, would put it in a better position to exert bigger influence on developments on the continent, thereby protecting its own security interests.

Conclusion

- South Africa must decide whether entering into an SPA with the EU is in its national interest. Its invocation of regional and multilateral commitments seem to indicate that it might have second thoughts.
- An SPA with the EU could negatively impact on South Africa's present relations with countries that are not aligned to the West or are anti-West. A strategic alliance with the EU would put South Africa firmly in the camp of the West, something it does not seem to want.
- A grand plan such as the suggested SPA comes over as bureaucratic heavy-handedness. South Africa might feel that the TDCA is in place and presents a good basis for "organic diplomacy"; that sound diplomatic and legal frameworks between the two parties do exist; dialogue does take place on a regular basis; and trade is booming. It seems unnecessary to change the diplomatic architecture so drastically.
- The EU should change its tactics in favour of a more patient and prudent brand of diplomacy. It should borrow from Robert Schuman's famous declaration of 9 May 1950 that "Europe will not be made all at once or according to a single plan. It will be built through concrete achievements which will first create real solidarity"[7]; or Jean Monnet's prudence when he explained the role of the European Coal and Steel Community: "The ECSC suggested a way of integrating Europe by stealth, without directly confronting the interests, offending the national sensibilities or compromising the identity of the existing nation state authorities... Little by little the work of the Community will be felt... Then the everyday realities will make it possible to

---

6   Statement by the Department of Foreign Affairs, Pretoria, 29 June 2006.
7   Cited in McCormick, p. 12.

form the political union which is the goal of our Community and to establish a United States of Europe... The unification of Europe, like all peaceful revolutions, takes time."[8] The EU's proposal does say that "partnership is not built overnight; it is the result of dynamic development". It seems to pre-empt dynamic development by coming forward with what could be interpreted as a teleological statement about future relations. A step-by-step approach of wise diplomacy and subtle manoeuvring usually produce better results.

- Apart from paternalism, which is so much disliked in the post-colonial African political culture, the Commission's proposal contains a strong dose of missionary revisionism, something South Africa might feel is superfluous, even assertive, bordering on EU interference in local decision-making. It is certainly in South Africa's national interest to invest more in its relationship. It should leave ideology and gripes about the past out of the equation. However, the rather clumsy, bulldozing way in which the EU has exercised its diplomacy in presenting this proposal for an SPA may be tactically unwise. But hopefully, the envisaged negotiations will produce a better basis for the elevation of the relationship, something that South Africa seems to be in favour of.[9]

---

8   Quoted in O'Neill, pp. 35, 36.
9   G. Olivier, "SA and the EU can build a partnership", *Business Day*, 24 August 2006, p. 19.

Selected Bibliography

ACP/EU Courier. 2000. Special Issue: Cotonou Agreement, pp. 6–10. Brussels: European Commission.

Adedeji, A. 2000. "From the Lagos Plan of Action to the New Partnership for Africa's Development, and from the Final Act of Lagos to the Constitutive Act: Whither Africa?" Conference paper, African Scholars Forum for Envisioning Africa, Nairobi.

Allen, D. & Byrne, P. 1985. "Multilateral decision-making and implementation: The case of the European Community". In Smith, S. & Clarke, M. (eds). *Foreign policy implementation*. London: Allen & Unwin.

Anyang' Nyong'o, P. 2002. "From the Lagos Plan of Action to Nepad: The dilemmas of progress in independent Africa". Conference paper, Renaissance South Africa Outreach Programme Continental Experts Meeting, Pretoria.

Archer, C. 2000. *The European Union: Structure and process*. London: Continuum.

Bertelsman-Scott, T., Mills, G. & Sidiropoulos, E. (eds). 2000. *The EU-SA agreement: South Africa, Southern Africa and the European Union*. Johannesburg: SA Institute for International Affairs.

Black, J. K. 1999. *Development in theory and practice: Paradigms and paradoxes*. Boulder: Westview.

Borchardt, K-D. 1994. *The ABC of Community law*. Luxembourg: Office of the Official Publications of the European Communities.

Bratton, M. & Landsberg, C. 1999. "From promise to delivery: Official development assistance to South Africa, 1994–8". Research report no. 68, ad hoc publication, University of the Witwatersrand Centre for Policy Studies, Johannesburg.

Burrows, B., Denton, G. & Edwards, G. (eds). 1977. *Federal solutions to European issues*. London: Macmillan.

Burtenshaw, J. "Afrikaners are embracing the new South Africa". *Beeld*, 25 May 2005, p. 14.

Business Day, 2 June 2003, p. 1.

Cafruny, A. W. & Lankovsky, C. (eds). 1997. *Europe's ambiguous unity: Conflict and consensus in the post-Maastricht era*. London: Lynne Rienner.

Chetty, V. "Positive spinoffs from the EU trade pact". *Business Day: Business Law Review*, February 2006, p. 5.

Cotonou Infokit, "The Cotonou Agreement at a glance (2)", (ECDPM 2001) <http://www.one world.org/ecdpm/en/Cotonou_gb.htm>, (p. 1), Maastricht, ECDPM.

Davies, R. 1990. "The Department of Trade and Industries perspective". Seminar report, South African Business and the European Union in the Context of the New Trade and Development Agreement, Rand Afrikaans University Centre for European Studies, Johannesburg.

Davies, R. "Forging a new relationship with the EU". In Bertelsman-Scott, T., Mills, G. & Sidiropoulos, E. (eds). 2000. *The EU-SA Agreement –*

South Africa, Southern Africa and the European Union. Johannesburg: SA Institute for International Affairs.

Delegation of the European Commission in South Africa. Annual Report. 1998. Pretoria.

Delegation of the European Commission in South Africa. Annual Report. 2001. Pretoria.

Delegation of the European Commission in South Africa. Annual Report. 2002. Pretoria.

Delegation of the European Commission in South Africa. Annual Report. 2004. Pretoria.

Department of Foreign Affairs, South Africa. Statement. 29 June 2006. Pretoria.

Devuyst, Y. 2003. *The European Union at the crossroads: The EU's institutional evolution from the Schuman Plan to the European Convention.* Brussels: P.I.E.-Peter Lang.

D'Souza, D. "Two cheers for colonialism". *Mail and Guardian*, 10–16 May 2002, pp. 30–31.

European Commission. 1994. "Southern Africa and the European Union", Series DE 78. Brussels: Directorate-general for Development.

European Commission. 1997. "Communication from the Commission to the European Council and the European Parliament on guidelines for the negotiation of new cooperation agreements with the African, Caribbean and Pacific (ACP) Countries". Brussels: Directorate-general for Development.

European Commission. 1999. "Country Strategy Paper for South Africa (2000–2002)". Brussels: Directorate-general for Development.

European Commission. 1999. "Partners in progress: The EU/South Africa Trade, Development and Cooperation Agreement for the 21st century". Brussels: Directorate Central Development.

European Commission. 1999. "The European Union and world trade". Brussels: Directorate-general for Information, Communication, Culture and Audiovisual Publications Unit.

European Commission. 2002. "Evaluation of the European Commission's Country Strategy for South Africa". Brussels: Directorate-general for Development.

European Commission. 2003. "South Africa-European Community Country Strategy Paper and Multi-annual Indicative Programme for the period 2003–2005". Pretoria: Directorate-general for Development.

European Commission. 2004. "Building an African-EU partnership for action". Discussion paper, Brussels.

European Commission. 2005. "How the European Union works: Your guide to the EU institutions". Luxembourg: Directorate-general for Press and Communications.

European Commission. 2006. "Communication from the Commission to the Council and the European Parliament: Towards an EU-South African Strategic Partnership." Brussels: Commission of the European Communities.

Faria, F. 2004. "Crisis management in sub-Saharan Africa: The role of the European Union". Occasional paper no. 51. Paris: Institute for Security Studies.

Fioramonti, L. 2003. "The European Community promoting human rights and democratic consolidation at micro-level: The case of South Africa". Conference paper, IPSA Conference, Durban.

Fioramonti, L. 2004. "The European Union promoting democracy in South Africa: Strengths and weaknesses". Conference paper, The Relationship between Africa and the European Union, University of the Western Cape, Cape Town.

Friedman, S. "Pan-African Parliament will be what its members make of it". *Business Day*, 29 September 2004, p. 12.

Gnesotto, N. (ed.) 2004. *EU Security and Defence Policy: The first five years (1999–2004)*. Paris: Institute for Security Studies.

Haas, E. B. 1958. *The uniting of Europe: Political, social and economic forces*. Palo Atto: Stanford University Press.

Haine, J-Y. "An historical perspective". In Gnesotto, N. (ed.) 2004. *EU Security and Defence Policy: The first five years (1999–2004)*. Paris: Institute for Security Studies.

Hanlon, J. & Ormond, R. 1987. *The sanctions handbook*. London: Harmondsworth.

Heller, P. S. 2005. "Making aid work", *Finance and Development*, 42:3, pp. 9–13.

Holland, M. 1988. *The European Community and South Africa*. London: Pinter.

Huntington, S. P. 1987. "The goals of development". In Weiner, M. & Huntington, S. P. (eds). *Understanding political development*. Boston: Little Brown.

Huntington, S. P. 1996. *The clash of civilizations and the remaking of world order*. New York: Simon & Shuster.

Jenkins, C. & Thomas, L. 2001. "African regionalism and the SADC". In Telo, M. (ed.) *European Union and New Regionalism: Regional actors and global governance in a post-hegemonic era*. Aldershot: Ashgate.

Jones, R. A. 2001. *The politics and economics of the European Union: An introductory text*. (2nd edn). Cheltenham: Edward Elgar.

Katzenellenbogen, J. "Nepad: The revolution in accountability". *Business Day*, 10 June 2002, p. 9.

Keet, D. "SA in dangerous waters with EU". *Mail and Guardian*, 29 January–4 February 1999, p. 12.

Kegley, C. W. (ed.) 1995. *Controversies in international relations theory, realism and the neo-liberal challenge*. New York: St Martins.

Konrad Adenauer Stiftung. 1999. Seminar report, South African Business and the European Union in the Context of the New Trade and Development Agreement, Johannesburg.

Laidler, M. 1998. "South Africa and the European Union: The Free Trade Agreement and Lomé – What can South Africa expect?" Seminar report, Europe and South Africa: A Productive Partnership into the Next Millennium, Rand Afrikaans University Centre for European Studies, Johannesburg.

Lake, M. 2003. "Putting the partnership into Nepad". Seminar paper, SA/EU Study Association, Pretoria.

Lee, M. C. 2002. "The European Union-South African Free Trade Agreement: In whose interest?" *Journal of Contemporary African Studies*, 20:1, pp. 82–106.
Leonard, M. "Why the US needs the EU". *Time*, 28 February 2005, p. 27.
Links, E. 1990. "The European Union-South Africa Trade, Development and Cooperation Agreement and Lomé: The implications". Seminar report, South African Business and the European Union in the Context of the New Trade and Development Agreement, Rand Afrikaans University Centre for European Studies, Johannesburg
Matshikiza, J. "A colonised intellect". *Mail and Guardian*, 17–22 May 2002, pp. 28–29.
Mbeki, T. 1996. "I am an African." Speech, South African Parliament, Cape Town.
Mbeki, T. 1997. "Africa's time has come." Speech, Corporate Council Summit, Chantilly, Virginia.
McCormick, J. 1999. *Understanding the European Union: A concise introduction*. London: Macmillan Press.
McGiffen, S. P. 2001. *The European Union: A critical guide*. London: Pluto.
Mohammed, A., Tesfagioris, P. & De Waal, A. 2001. "Peace and security dimensions of the African Union". Ad hoc background paper for AFD 111. Addis Ababa: Economic Commission for Africa.
Moravcsic, A. 1988. "Negotiating the Single European Act: National interests and conventional statecraft in the European Community". In Nelsen, B. F. & Stubb, A. C-G. (eds). *The European Union: Readings on the theory and practice of European integration*. London: Lynne Rienner.
Morgenthau, H. J. 1973. *Politics among nations: The struggle for power and peace*. New York: Alfred A. Knopf.
Nelsen, B. F. & Stubb, A. C-G. (eds). 1988. *The European Union: Readings on the theory and practice of European integration*. London: Lynne Rienner.
Nielson, P. 2000. "The new agreement will benefit the poorest". *ACP/EU Courier*, Special Issue: Cotonou Agreement, p. 3.
Nugent, N. 1999. *The government and politics of the European Union*. London: Macmillan.
O'Neill, M. 1996. *The politics of European integration: Political, social and economic forces*. London: Routledge.
Olivier, G. 2003. "Is Thabo Mbeki Africa's saviour?" *International Affairs*, 79:4, pp. 815–828.
Olivier, G. "Costly allure of pied piper of ideology". *Business Day*, 30 January 2004, p. 9.
Olivier, G. "One plan will not fit all Africa". *Business Day*, 7 February 2005, p. 12.
Olivier, G. "SA and the EU can build a partnership". *Business Day*, 24 August 2006, p. 19.
Olivier, M. 2002. "Development cooperation agreements between the EU, its member states and SA: An assessment of the legal requirements". Conference paper, ECSASA Conference, University of the Western Cape, Cape Town.

Ortega, M. 2004. "Global views on the European Union". Challiot paper, no. 72. Paris: European Union Institute for Security Studies.
Powell, K. 2005. *Opportunities and challenges for delivering on the responsibility to protect the African Union's emerging peace and security regime*. Ottawa: The North–South Institute.
Pretoria News, 25 February 2004, p. 5.
Pretoria News: Business Report, 13 February 2006, p. 17
Prodi, R. 2002. "A wider Europe: A proximity policy as the key to stability". Speech, Sixth ECSA-World Conference, Brussels.
Richardson, J. (ed.) 1996. *European Union: Power and policy-making*. London: Routledge.
Schepers, S. 2003. "Missing chances in Europe?" *Leadership Magazine* 249, pp. 31–32.
Schreiner, W. 2002. "Press coverage in South Africa on the European Union". Conference paper, SA/EU workshops under the auspices of the Centre for European Studies, Rand Afrikaans University, Johannesburg.
Sidiripoulos, E. (ed.) 2001. *A continent apart: Kosovo, Africa and humanitarian intervention*. Johannesburg: SA Institute for International Affairs.
Smalberger, W. 2000. "Lessons learnt by South Africa during the negotiations". In Bertelsman-Scott, T., Mills, G. & Sidiropoulos, E. (eds). *The EU-SA Agreement – South Africa, Southern Africa and the European Union*. Johannesburg: SA Institute for International Affairs.
Smidt, S. 1996. "The EU's support for regional cooperation and economic integration in Southern Africa". Conference paper, AWEPA Conference on Reconstruction and Democratisation in Southern Africa, Cape Town.
Solana, J. 2002. *A secure Europe in a better world*. Paris: European Union Institute for Security Studies.
Solana, J. 2004. "Preface". In Gnesotto, N. (ed.) *EU Security and Defence Policy: The first five years (1999–2004)*. Paris: Institute for Security Studies.
Stevens, C. & Kennan, J.,with Fischer, S., Roberts, G. & Rudy, R. 1995. "Trade between South Africa and Europe: Future prospects and policy choices". Working paper, University of Sussex Institute of Developing Studies, Brighton.
Sunday Times: Business Times, Johannesburg, 28 May 2006, p. 4
Telo, M. (ed.) 2001. *European Union and New Regionalism: Regional actors and global governance in a post-hegemonic era*. Aldershot: Ashgate.
Thompson, V. B. 1969. *Africa and unity: The evolution of pan-Africanism*. London: Longman.
Towards True Partnership: EU-Africa Summit – A CIDSE Position Paper. <http://www.cidse.org/pubs/euafpt2.htm>, p. 1.
Van der Westhuyzen, C. 2004. "Africa and the changing face of the EU: Economic opportunity or threat?" *Global Insight* 39, pp. 1–9.
Weidenfeld, W. & Wessels, W. 1997. *Europe from A to Z: Guide to European integration*. Luxemburg: Institut für Europäische Politik.
Weiner, M. & Huntington, S. P. 1987. *Understanding political development*. Boston: Little Brown.

Welch, C. E. 1992. "The African Commission on Human and Peoples' Rights: A five year report and assessment". *Human Rights Quarterly*, 14, p. 43.

Wikipedia, "Africa Union". 2006. <C:%20Union%20-20-%20Wikipedia, %20 the%20%free%2Encyclopedia.htm>

Wikipedia, "Image. EU map." 2006. <http://en.wikipedia.org/wik/ Image: EU_map_names_isles.png>

Wolpert, S. 2001. *Gandhi's passion: The life and legacy of Mahatma Gandhi*. Oxford: Oxford University Press.

World Bank. 1981. "Accelerated development in sub-Saharan Africa: An agenda for action". Washington D.C.

Index

ACP countries, 30, 31, 37, 47–51, 59, 60, 90, 144, 165, 168
  development aid, 47, 62, 90
  indebtedness, 47, 61
  politics, 48, 52, 58
  trade, 47, 48, 60, 61, 149
ACP/EU Committee of Ambassadors, 59
ACP/EU Council, 59
ACP/EU Joint Assembly, 59
ACP/EU relationship, 31, 46, 62, 63, 66, 77, 94
  See also Cotonou Agreement, Lomé Conventions, Yaoundé Agreement
acquis communautaire, 100
Adedeji, Adebayo, 150
Africa
  ideology, 146
  integration, 96, 99
  politics, 131
  poverty, 43
Africa Commission, 54
Africa-Europe Summit, 127, 149
Africa rescue plans, 142, 144, 148, 153
African Charter on Human and Peoples' Rights, 120, 136
African Commission on Human and Peoples' Rights, 120, 137
African Court on Human and Peoples' Rights, 120, 136
African Peer Review Mechanism, 99, 104, 135, 137, 139, 146, 147, 150
African Renaissance, 63, 98, 135, 141, 142, 150, 159
  See also Mbeki, Thabo
African Special Programmes, 148
African Union, 79, 93, 98, 132, 133, 156
  Assembly, 106, 110, 119, 120, 133, 135
  Commission, 120
  Constitutive Act, 95, 99, 104, 110, 112, 118, 119, 120, 132, 133, 136, 137
  Court of Justice, 120
  decision-making and voting, 111–112
  defence and security, 125, 130–136
  economic development, 105
  Executive Council, 110
  integration, 103–106, 112, 114, 132, 137, 138
  leadership, 141
  legal framework, 110, 115, 118–120
  membership, 99, 100, 119, 146
  Peace and Security Agenda, 145
  Peace and Security Council, 104, 127, 133, 134, 136
  political character, 99, 100, 103, 114, 121, 138
  structural features, 105–107
  See also NEPAD
Africanisation, 14
Afrikaner, 14, 19, 25, 26
  nationalism, 19, 20, 22, 25, 26
Afrocentrism, 13, 14, 15, 20, 63, 146, 159
Afro-Europeanism, 14
aid fatigue, 55, 163, 164
al-Qaddafi, Muammar, 137
ANC, 14, 17, 20, 26, 30, 63, 159, 160, 169
  post-apartheid ideology, 63, 83, 159
Anglo-Boer War, 16, 19, 26
apartheid, 15, 16, 18, 19, 20, 23, 91, 98, 99, 159, 160, 161, 165
  anti-apartheid action, 30, 31, 32, 62
  demise, 31, 33, 57, 62, 70, 77
  EU and apartheid SA, 24–34
  regime, 159

SA isolation, 16, 23, 25, 26, 27, 28, 57, 70, 122
sanctions, 2333, 82, 85, 158–160
victims of apartheid, 31–33, 57, 62, 67, 78, 82, 83, 85, 160, 165
Aristide, Jean-Bertrand, 159
Arusha conference, 147, 149
asymmetry in EU/SA relationship, 66, 67, 156, 157, 161

Belgium, 27, 42, 78, 108
Berg Report, 147, 149
Berlusconi, Sylvio, 81
Boer, 16, 19
Bouteflika, Abdelaziz, 142
Britain, 16, 155
　Anglo-Boer War, 26
　anti-British sentiments, 26
　colonialism, 16, 17, 19, 22, 23, 46
　involvement in SA, 16, 19, 20, 23, 27
　See also United Kingdom
Brittan, Leon, 58
Burundi, 49, 79, 127, 135, 139, 147

Caetano, Marcelo, 100
Cairo Declaration, 149, 151
Cape of Good Hope, 13, 16, 17, 21
Carter, Jimmy, 28
Central Europe, 168
Charlemagne, 96
Churchill, Winston, 40
Cold War, 22, 24, 62, 77, 98, 126, 150
　post-Cold War, 41, 47, 90
colonialism, 16–23, 25, 98, 146, 148, 150
　anti-colonialism, 21, 23
　by Britain, 16, 17, 19, 22, 23, 46
　by France, 16
　by the Netherlands, 16–19, 22
　colonizers, 17, 19, 90, 131
　demise, 22, 25, 97, 131
　guerrilla struggles, 99, 131
　neo-colonialism, 18, 146
　of ACP states, 31
　of Africa, 130, 131, 152
　of North America, 17
　post-colonialism, 77, 104, 131, 136

Common African Defence and Security Policy, 132, 133, 134, 135
Commonwealth, 16, 19, 26, 27, 28
Concert of Europe, 96
confederalism, 37, 38, 41, 101, 102, 114
　See also intergovernmentalism, statecentrism
Conference, Workshop and Cultural Initiative Fund, 81
Côte d'Ivoire, 49, 98, 127, 135, 137
Cotonou Agreement, 16, 45, 46, 48, 51, 52, 53, 54, 77, 79, 87, 90, 93, 94, 144, 146, 149, 150, 151, 152, 160, 167
　See also ACP/EU relationship
Coudenhove-Kalergie, Count, 97
Council of Europe, 126
Council of Foreign Ministers, 29, 30, 32, 33, 38, 58, 61, 107, 108, 111, 115, 124, 128, 160
　functional configurations and functions, 111

Darfur, 135, 139
Davies, Robert, 89
Delors, Jacques, 139
Democratic Republic of the Congo, 49, 79, 127, 135, 137, 147
Denmark, 24, 27, 28, 42, 78, 108
Dias, Bartholomeu, 13, 16, 18
Dutch East Indian Company, 16, 17, 18

Eastern Europe, 28, 62, 146, 168
Economic Commission for Africa, 147, 149
Economic integration, 120–22
Economic Partnership Agreement, 48, 51
ECOWAS, 121, 122, 127, 138
English, 14
Euratom, 105, 114
Eurocentrism, 13, 14, 15, 18, 20, 21, 22, 63, 83, 146, 159
　See also westernization
Europe
　integration, 96, 99
　involvement in SA, 13, 15, 31

European Central Bank, 106, 108
European Coal and Steel Community, 101, 102, 105, 112, 114, 121, 122, 125, 140
European Commission, 26, 31, 33, 38, 51, 52, 53, 54, 59, 77, 89, 91, 105, 107, 108, 111, 115, 116, 124, 128, 140, 151, 155, 161, 168, 169
   development aid, 145
   individual members, 44
   policy making, 36, 38
European Community, 20, 24, 27, 31, 33, 38, 78, 102
   Code of Conduct, 28, 29
   development aid to SA, 32, 33
   development policies, 31, 148, 149
   diplomatic delegation to South Africa, 78, 79, 162, 167
   domestic policy, 85
   economic integration, 124
   foreign policy, 26, 29
   individual members, 24, 28, 46
   institututions, 116
   legal framework, 100, 102
   philosophy, 101
   relationship with SA, 28, 30, 33
   sanctions, 26, 27, 28, 31
   structural features, 115, 117, 118
   See also European Economic Community, European Union
European Common Foreign and Security Policy, 38, 85, 111, 127–130, 133
European Council, 38, 39, 54, 58, 59, 73, 87, 99, 102, 105, 107, 108, 111, 115, 116, 127, 128
European Court of Justice, 38, 105, 106, 107, 115
European Economic and Monetary Union, 125
European Economic and Social Committee, 53, 54
European Economic Community, 20, 46, 47, 105, 112, 114, 123
   See also European Community, European Union
European Monetary System, 125
European Parliament, 38, 54, 59, 87, 100, 105, 107, 108, 111, 115, 116, 140
   functions, 111
European Programme for Reconstruction and Development, 32, 72, 73, 74, 75, 76, 81
European Security and Defence Policy, 128, 129, 130
European Security Strategy, 39, 40, 128
European Union, 20, 33, 42, 90, 122, 162
   affluence, 85, 89
   characteristics, 96, 168
   Common Agricultural Policy, 36, 47, 55, 67, 68, 84, 90, 91, 123
   Copenhagen criteria, 100
   Country Strategy Paper for South Africa, 33, 87
   decision-making and voting, 107–111
   development aid, 32, 37, 46, 47, 51, 52, 55, 59, 62, 85, 87, 89, 90, 154, 157
   development aid to SA, 57, 75, 83, 85–87, 89, 91, 156, 161–167
   development policy, 35, 41, 44, 45–56, 52, 77, 85, 93, 143
   domestic policy, 99, 140, 168
   economic cooperation with SA, 82
   enlargement, 36, 40, 47, 62, 100, 102, 114, 122, 126, 127, 146, 168
   foreign policy, 35, 39, 41, 84, 86, 88, 90, 91, 154, 156, 168
   Growth and Stability Pact, 146
   integration, 37–42, 94, 99, 100, 101, 104, 112, 113, 114, 121, 123–125, 137, 138, 139, 153
   involvement in Africa, 80, 93–95, 122, 135, 137, 146
   involvement in SA, 35, 65, 82, 85, 87, 92, 157, 167, 169
   legal framework, 38, 107, 108, 113, 115–118
   membership, 41, 42, 99, 100, 102, 104

peace and security initiatives in Africa, 127
policy making, 38, 102
policy towards NEPAD, 141, 142–145, 146, 164
policy towards SA, 57, 58, 84–92, 86, 155, 157, 161, 168
political character, 36, 37, 39, 41, 44, 113, 114
self-interest, 83, 84, 85, 86, 88, 89, 90, 91
single market, 47, 68, 114, 123
structural features, 38, 105–107
trade, 36, 37, 43, 65, 91, 92, 94
trade with ACP countries, 47, 58
trade with SA, 67, 156, 157
See also European Community, European Economic Community
eurosclehrosis, 101, 121
Exchange Rate Mechanism, 125

fascism, 25
Federal Europe, *See* United States of Europe
federalism, 37, 38, 39, 41, 97, 101, 102, 114
See also functionalism, multilateralism, supranationalism
Fortress Europe, 84, 90, 168
France, 24, 27, 39, 42, 72, 78, 101, 102, 108, 124, 130, 155, 158
colonialism, 16
French Revolution, 96
Franco, Francisco, 100
Free Trade Agreement, 15, 58, 60, 67, 68, 69, 70, 86, 91
Free Trade Area, 59, 61
See also Trade, Development and Cooperation Agreement
Free Trade Zone, *See* Free Trade Area
functionalism, 38, 101, 102, 121
See also federalism, multilateralism, supranationalism

G7, 122
G8, 39, 42, 44, 54, 55, 56, 141, 142, 145, 146, 151, 155, 164
Evian meeting, 145

Germany, 24, 27, 42, 72, 78, 101, 108, 124, 125, 158
Nazi Germany, 23, 25
Giscard d'Estaing, Valéry, 39
Great Lakes Area, 80, 127
Guribab, Theo-Ben, 147

Haider, Jörg, 105
Highly Indebted Poor Country Programmes, 148
HIV/AIDS, 54, 55, 68, 73, 75, 79, 80, 136, 166, 169
Houphouët-Boigny, Félix, 98
Howe, Godfrey, 30, 160

idea of Africa, 96, 97
idea of Europe, 96, 97
imperialism, 16, 19, 25, 98
Inter-American Courts, 120
intergovernmentalism, 26, 37, 38, 39, 41, 102, 103, 104, 105, 106, 107, 110, 113, 114, 115, 121, 126, 129, 133, 137, 139
See also confederalism, statecentrism
International Monetary Fund, 132, 142
Ireland, 24, 27, 28, 42, 60, 78, 108, 124
Italy, 24, 27, 29, 42, 78, 81, 108, 158

Joint South African-European Union Science and Technology Cooperation Committee, 81

Kananaskis Action Plan, 145
Kananaskis G8 summit, 152
Kant, Immanuel, 96, 138
Kosovo, 129

Lagos Plan of Action, 147, 148, 149
Laidler, Michael, 64, 65
Lake, Michael, 143
Latin America, 28, 37
Lomé Conventions, 30, 31, 45, 46, 47, 48, 51, 52, 58, 59, 60, 61, 63, 64, 66, 77, 90, 143, 144, 149, 151, 160
See also ACP/EU relationship
Luxembourg, 28, 29, 42, 79, 108

Macmillan, Harold, 27
Mandela, Nelson, 20, 30, 141, 160
Mandelson, Peter, 142
Marshall Aid, 165
Mbeki, Thabo, 58, 98, 137, 141, 142, 145, 146, 150, 161
  See also African Renaissance
Millennium Development Goals, *See* United Nations: Millennium Development Goals
Mitrany, David, 101
Monnet, Jean, 82, 101, 103, 139, 173
Mubarak, Hosni, 142
Mugabe, Robert, 80, 104, 146
multilateralism, 37, 39, 40, 43, 138
  See also federalism, functionalism, supranationalism

National Party, 16, 19, 20, 22, 25
NATO, 39, 126, 128, 130
neo-colonialism, 18, 146
NEPAD, 54, 74, 79, 93, 94, 99, 104, 105, 112, 121, 122, 135, 139, 141–153, 164
Netherlands, the, 24, 27, 29, 39, 42, 78, 102, 108, 130
  colonialism, 16–19, 22
Nielsen, Poul, 151
Nkrumah, Kwame, 97, 141
Non-Aligned Movement, 26, 141
North and South American integration, 104, 122
North-South divide, 41, 45, 91, 141, 157
Nyong'o, Anyang', 150

Obasanjo, Olusegun, 142
Official Development Assistance, 33, 37, 42, 47, 55, 62, 76, 78, 85, 86, 88, 89, 144, 148, 154, 162, 163, 164, 165, 166, 168
Organisation for African Unity, 26, 95, 98
  Charter, 99
  dysfunctionality, 98
  philosophy, 98, 103
  structural features, 106

Pan-African Parliament, 105, 106, 110, 139, 140
pan-Africanism, 20, 97, 98, 99, 138, 139, 141
neo-pan-Africanism, 141
Pan-European Movement, 97
pan-Europeanism, 37
partnership
  ACP/EU, 48, 51, 53, 149, 151
  African, 142, 146, 151, 152
  development paradigm, 18, 152, 153
  EU/AU, 151
  EU/NEPAD, 144, 145, 146
  EU/SA, 15, 65, 81, 82, 156, 158, 161, 165, 169
  EU/SA strategic partnership, 158, 159–161, 167, 168
  global partnership for devolopment, 54
  Third World, 40
pax Americana, 42
Pisani Memorandum, 46, 149
political dialogue
  in Cotonou Agreement, 48, 51
  under TDCA, 78–81, 137
Prodi, Romano, 39, 140
Putin, Vladimir, 81

Qualified Majority Voting, 108, 110

racism, 19, 22, 25, 98, 141, 157
Rapid Reaction Force, 126, 128, 130
Reconstruction and Development Programme, 33
regionalization, 48, 53, 91, 96, 104, 121, 139
  Africa, 94, 95, 104, 112, 121, 135
  EU, 104
Russia, 40, 81, 168
Rwanda, 50, 132, 143, 147

SA/EU
  economic relationship, 57–78
  partnership, 15, 65, 81, 82, 83, 156, 158, 161, 165, 169
  relationship, 13, 15, 16, 20, 34, 36, 44, 57, 58, 63, 65, 66, 142, 154–156, 158, 160, 162, 167, 168, 169

strategic partnership, 91, 158, 159–161, 167, 168
sanctions
  against apartheid SA, 23, 25–33, 82, 85, 158
  against Zimbabwe, 80
  by AU, 110, 119
  by EU, 159, 160
  by EC, 33, 36
  by UN, 25, 26, 28, 82
  military sanctions, 32
Schengen Agreement, 124
  Benelux countries, 124
Schuman, Robert, 99, 101, 139, 173
Scientific Cooperation Agreement, 167
Single European Act, 108, 114, 116, 123
Single European Market, 123
Sirte, 132, 135, 137
Smidt, Steffen, 60
Smuts, Jan Christiaan, 25, 26
Solana, Javier, 36, 128
South Africa, 16
  colonialism, 13–23, 25, 31, 63
  economy, 59, 62, 67, 70, 73, 91
  foreign policy, 13, 15, 80, 92, 141, 155, 161, 169
  ideology, 14, 15, 63, 64, 83, 157, 159, 161, 167, 168, 169
  involvement in Africa, 93, 95, 121, 135, 137, 157
  NEPAD, 142, 143
  politics, 32, 57, 62, 77, 80, 82, 89, 93, 137, 158, 165
  role in SADC, 59, 61, 68, 77, 79, 83, 87
  trade with EU, 67, 86, 156, 161, 168
  Union of South Africa, 19
  World War 2, 25
Southern African Customs Union, 68, 69, 93, 94, 122, 138
Southern African Development Community, 61, 68, 69, 71, 76, 79, 93, 94, 120, 121, 122, 127, 138
Southern African Development Coordination Conference, 30, 32
Spaak, Paul Henri, 101, 139

statecentrism, 41, 44, 85, 100, 101, 102, 103, 104, 121, 126, 133, 140
  See also confederalism, intergovernmentalism
St-Malo Declaration, 128
Structural Adjustment Programmes, 142, 147, 149
sub-Saharan Africa, 20, 22, 51, 121, 130, 148
supranationalism, 37, 38, 41, 44, 97, 100, 101, 102, 103, 105, 107, 112, 113, 114, 115, 121, 123, 126, 133, 137, 139
  See also federalism, functionalism, multilateralism

Third World, 26, 44, 63, 77, 85, 91, 141
  against apartheid SA, 26, 28
  aid, 164
  politics, 63
  poverty, 47, 56, 85
Thompson, Vincent Bakpetu, 97
Trade, Development and Cooperation Agreement, 16, 57, 59, 61, 62–82, 65, 78, 79, 82, 83, 87, 89, 91, 92, 94, 137, 158, 160, 161, 162, 165, 167, 168
  Fisheries Agreement, 65, 67
  Free Trade Area, 59
  political dialogue, 64, 78–81, 137
  Science and Technology Agreement, 67
  Wine and Spirits Agreement, 65, 67, 167
    regional brand names, 65, 68, 89
Treaty
  Draft Constitutional, 39, 40, 41
  ECSC, *See* Treaty of Rome
  of Amsterdam, 45, 102, 108, 113, 114, 116, 124, 127, 128
  of Maastricht, 38, 45, 101, 102, 108, 113, 114, 116, 125, 126, 127, 148
  of Nice, 102, 114
  of Paris, 101, 102, 110, 114, 125
  of Rome, 30, 102, 108, 114, 117, 122, 123

of the European Union, *See* Treaty of Maastricht
Troika Diplomatic Mission, 29

ubuntu, 15, 104
United Kingdom, 21, 24, 27, 28, 29, 39, 41, 42, 46, 54, 72, 74, 78, 102, 108, 124, 130, 158
See also Britain
United Nations, 26, 27, 28, 39, 40, 54, 55, 78, 88, 102, 115, 132, 135, 142, 144, 147, 148, 149, 156
   arms embargo, 28
   Charter, 40, 98, 129
   Development Decade, 148
   Millennium Development Goals, 53, 54, 55, 152
   sanctions, 25, 26, 82
   Security Council, 27, 39
United States of Africa, 137
United States of America, 28, 37, 39, 40, 41, 42, 63, 72, 74, 78, 97, 123, 125, 128, 130, 155, 159, 162
   trade, 37
United States of Europe, 40, 96, 97, 101, 154

Wade, Abdoulaye, 142
Washington consensus, 90, 146, 150
Western European Union, 126, 128, 130
westernization, 18, 22, 81, 159
See also Eurocentrism
Westphalian paradigm, 39, 40, 41, 98, 100, 104, 138
Wilson, Woodrow, 39
Wilsonian paradigm, 39
World Bank, 78, 132, 142, 147, 148, 149
World Health Organisation, 94
World Trade Organisation, 51, 60, 67, 69, 78, 142, 145
World War 1, 16, 39, 97
World War 2, 16, 21, 22, 23, 24, 25, 97, 101, 125

Yaoundé Agreement, 30, 46, 142, 149
See also ACP/EU relationship

Zimbabwe, 50, 79, 80, 104, 135, 137, 146, 147, 159, 166